A CALL FROM THE BEYOND

A CALL FROM THE BEYOND

A Book Dedicated to You

Volume Two

Narinder Bhandari

PARTRIDGE

To order additional copies of this book, contact
Partridge India
000 800 10062 62
orders.india@partridgepublishing.com

www.partridgepublishing.com/india

Dedication and Acknowledgements:

This Book is dedicated to the 'Self', the Self that is the 'self' in all . . . to Your 'self'.

Narinder deeply acknowledges the debt he owes to his mother for sowing the seeds of spiritualism in him at a very tender age. To his Father, for sowing the seeds of selflessness and service.

I am also indebted to my wife Ravi for being a constant source of inspiration through my life.

Finally, thanks to my son Karan for helping me edit the final version of this book.

Contents

BIOGRAPHY

Narinder Bhandari, 76, is a retired Army Officer, and lives in Chandigarh, INDIA with his wife Ravi, son Karan and family.

The greatest 'happening' in his lifetime, says he, was "The Death of Time for one single Moment in 1982; a gift of his Guru, God and Meditation. Past and Future ceased to exist. Life became a spontaneous living in the Light of awareness of the present Moment.

Of that experience, Narinder expresses in the following words:

The Death of Time is the Death of the Mind.

The ensuing Silence is TOTAL.

That Silence, sudden-like, becomes a sound... a Sound that is itself Light... or is it the other way around...

The darkness of Mind, in throes of death, gives Birth to a Light so dazzling that the eyes close in ecstasy ... and in the ears rings the Music of the following words ....

"Anand bhaya meri Mayee, Satguru mein Paya"

(Bliss, O my Beloved mother,
The Satguru has removed the veil between HIM and Me, to reveal Himself to me!

Ah, BLISS, truly has become My Being

Narinder, now, is the Satguru's disciple!)

Ah, how the Music resonates...!!!

Poetry began to arise in my Consciousness in 1998.

Words that have been heard thousands of times before, are now words NO MORE. The Words are the Light. The Words are the Sound.

As for the use of a capital letter for the names narinder and Nari in my writings... I use a small 'n' for narinder, signifying Humility of an un-awakened narinder; and, I use a capital 'N' in Nari, to indicate that Nari stands for an awakened Narinder...

The small n and the Capital N distinguish the state of Mind...

PREFACE TO VOLUME ONE

Sri Narinder Bhandari has written a truly marvellous book based on his own spiritual experience, rather than from dry pedantry or arid scholastic theory, in order to lead and help any sincere, earnest aspirant wishing to achieve the highest aim that any man or woman can ever have, that of Self or God Realisation.

In this fine book Narinder simply clarifies and explains what is actually meant by these hallowed terms 'God' and 'Self Realisation', in clear and simple language. He teaches an effective method of Meditation, mapping out the necessary path to achieve this art, and clearly defines the desired Goal to be reached.

In addition he fully examines the meaning of the term Guru, and his or her place needed in the great spiritual journey to Self Realisation. He also examines the sacred relationship to be achieved with God through Prayer, and then succinctly explains the correct understanding of what is meant by ones Karma and Destiny.

Finally, in delightful chapters he digresses on the True Art of Love and Marriage leading to an ideal life of happily fulfilled Dharma.

I heartily recommend this book to the earnest aspirant for its clarity and advice, which are genuinely based on the Authors own Spiritual Experience.

Alan Jacobs
President of the Ramana Maharshi Foundation UK

PREFACE TO VOLUME TWO

This fine book is never ever dull reading. Sri Narinder Bhandari gives to all spiritual aspirants very great advice, based on his own undoubted experience, and he is always essentially practical. He emphasises beyond any doubt that the True Purpose of Life is Self or God Realisation.

In this book he discusses the Ultimate Task of posing the Great Question of 'Who Am i?', the practice which leads to Real Happiness, the main purpose of our life.

He also discusses the important question as to whether or not Destiny can be changed?, and pays humble tribute to the inspiration and help he has received from the Great Sages, Guru Nanak, Sri Ramana Maharshi and Sri Nisagadatta Maharaj.

Among many other topics which are poetically discussed, are Meditation, Love, Self Knowledge, and many many more. He himself became Enlightened in1982, and stresses that All Higher Religions issue from the Great One God. He also tells us how to conquer the subtle demonic Ego which has cunningly usurped the place of the Divine Self in our daily living.

This is only a brief summary of this masterly book. There is much more there in these pages, and as a Poet himself, he delights us with extracts from the Great Kabir concerning Consciousness and Spiritual Energy, along with some of his own inspiring verses.

As a personal generous gift he gives us his E Mail Address and Telephone Number, so he is able to correspond, or speak with Devotees who are having difficulties with their spiritual progress and need guidance.. He even offers an opportunity for a personal meeting.

One can do no more than heartily recommend this truly excellent book for all those spiritually minded souls who are aspiring for their own Realisation of the Immortal Divine Self.

Alan Jacobs,
President Ramana Maharshi Foundation UK.

Here I give the words of Swami Chinmayananada, who used them for the Spiritual Books he had written:

WHAT TO DO WITH THIS BOOK

~ Swami Chinmayananda

Vedanta is a Science and so it must be studied in a systematic way. Don't try to read through; this is not a novel or something of semi-heavy reading. This book is for the students to reflect upon, all by themselves. So don't read more than5 to 10 pages a day. Read slowly, carefully, noting all the ideas developed therein..

As you read thus, a lot of tiny doubts will arise in your mind; sometimes you may question the very logic of certain conclusions in what you read. Please note them all down in a notebook, kept separate for this purpose. Clearly express your doubts. After having recorded your doubts forget them, and continue reading your daily quota of pages.

On the following Sunday, or on any holiday when you have some spare time, please take up the note-book, and a pencil in hand. Start reading your own doubts collected during the week. You will find surprisingly that you can check off many of the doubts because you have already the answers in you. The week's reading has widened your vision.

Maybe there are some questions to which you do not have the answers.

Leave them alone. From Monday continue the regular program of daily study, and recording all doubts whenever they arise in your bosom. Repeat checking up all the back-log of unanswered doubts. By the time you come tothe end of the book, you will find that all your questions are answered.

Go slow. There is no hurry. Your independent thinking is of utmost importance. Don't blindly believe; question every statement; accept no action as greater than your own understanding. Then alone can we enter into the Science of Vedanta ; then alone our knowledge can unfold our Self.

TRY. YOU CAN; YOU MUST: You owe it to yourself.

From Volume 1

AND SO OFTEN, IT HAPPENS THAT...

I pick up the pen
And, watch words and letters appear as writing
So, too, the Pen and the Parchment, I see
But I am struck with awe
The writer is nowhere to be found.
I think of my Beloved
The Beloved I have never seen
And the heart says,
"It could only be Him
Yes, it could only be Him, the writer
Who is nowhere to be found"
~narinder
Musings...
If you were the writer, Lord
Were you also the Pen and the Parchament?
All? Or, were you beyond
The witness invisible
Were you the moving finger
Or, the mind behind it
Both? Or, were you beyond
The witness invisible
Were you the Creation, Lord
Or, were you the Creator
Both, or neither, or, were you beyond

The witness invisible
Were you the self, pining and forlorn
Or the Self really you, the forgetful actor
Or, yet beyond were you, Lord
The witness invisible
Were you the Unity of Existence, Lord
Or were you the two-ness of the manifest
Or yet beyond
The witness invisible
And beloved
Are you the questing spirit
The eternal question
Or, the One answer, death to the Question
Or are you beyond,
The silent laughter
The Light of lights, beyond all darkness
Art thou Lord
Or, art thou the Sound of Sounds, the Soundless sound
Or, are you the thundering silence
Of the witness invisible
Are you the suffering sorrow, Lord
Or, are you the ecstasy of bliss divine
Or, beyond bliss and sorrow
The witness unknowable
Every question is itself the answer
Each answer a begging question.
Neither question, nor answer, are you Lord
Only the teasing silence
Of the witness beyond.
The writing has come to an end, Lord
The pen has stopped
The writer is still a mystery
The transcendence beyond.

PS: This was the first Poem that flowed from narinder's heart, in the year 1998.

Was it not indicating to him that the poetry that is going to be penned by him, is NOT written by him... it is Existence's Gift to him... he need not become unduly arrogant!

After the poem above, there was a spate of flow of poetry, in different languages; Punjabi, Hindi English. Words that had been heard thousands of times before, are now words NO MORE.

The Words have become the Light. The Words have become the Sound.

AUM

THE PURPOSE OF LIFE

The Purpose of Life is Self-Realisation, or God-Realisation. This human body has been given to you.

This is your chance to meet the Lord of the Universe.

All Other Work you do, will not work.

Join the Saadh Sangat, the Company of the Holy; vibrate and meditate on the Jewel of the Naam.
And, thus Realise the Truth of your Being.

AUM

What does a Guru do?

The Guru gives you the answers, for he knows... he has 'known' that essence... the essence abides in him... and he himself is the 'essence' of the words... the 'Being' is him... Verily he knows... and he answers...

And one day... some day... his look, his smile, his words answer the ultimate Question... the ultimate Question, 'who am I?'...
And as his words, his answer, his Being enters your Being... His answer becomes your answer...
One day... someday, you 'know'... and when you know, all questions drop... all questions disappear... and you smile... you smile... and your smile is the smile of knowing...

You have Realised yourself.

AUM

narinder's TWO Gurus...

Sant Paranpal Singh of Jhansi: The Sage responsible for narinder's Awakening.

The Gurudeva that Beloved Krishna made available to narinder in 1960, when he was 21.

His Blessings, in a spontaneous surge of Love... reduced the long period, and many steps, of narinder's Sadhna...

Air Commodore (Retd) Mohinder Singh, who came into narinder's Life in 1977, taught narinder Meditation, took him deeper into it, to lead him into Samadhi in 1982.

AUM

Volume Two

We begin with the Purpose of Life...

Happiness that does not wax and wane... What could be a better Purpose of Life?

And, where do we end?

Becoming aware of the turmoil and strife in one's life, the Seeker began with the Purpose of Life, prayed for the Guru, walked earnestly under the guidance of the Enlightened Master, meditated on the Naam, and... where did he end up?

With NO more Goals... the Moment Now itself the Destination, abidance therein. NO Purpose of Life any more.

This Moment NOW, the Eternal Moment itself flowering into ordained activity for the remaining days of the Body's life... winding up the remaining Accounts with all those around him...

The Sage's primary activity - of the nature of non-activity, for it accrues NO Karma, is teaching Other Seekers how to reach the Goal of Life or 'the Purpose of Life.'

AUM

Inspiration from my father

It was past midnight on a cold wintry night., in Shimla.

The doctor was himself lying in the bed, with high Fever.

Suddenly the phone rang. It was a call from a sick patient, asking for the doctor to come. The doctor began to get up. His wife asked him not to do so, he was himself sick, and the patient lived in deep ravine far away. Besides, he was a poor man, and never paid the docor's fees.

But, the doctor refused to listen to his wife, got up, called his assistant, who lived in a room upstairs, and picked up his doctor's bag containing essential Medicines.

This was a story repeated many a time. The same pleadings from his wife; and his refusing to listen to her.

He not only, would go, but would often give Free medicines to the poor patients, unable to afford the Treatment.

The Doctor was Narinder's Father, Dr Iqbal Singh.

His conduct, Narinder never did forget; and would himself always help the Needy, whether for the education of a child, or for his Treatment, or that of a member of his family.

Gods's Grace flowed on Narinder 's head, further enhanced by his two Gurus, till one day, guided by them, he reached Enlightenment.

And now, he teaches others the path to enlightenment.

AUM

Inspiration from my mother

My Mother, Premlata Bhandari, who sowed the seeds of Spiritualism in me, when I was an infant of 5 or 6. She read out every night to me, stories from Ramayana, Mahahbharta, and the Stories of the Ten Gurus of the Sikhs.

The Faith that she inspired in me, went on to become Meditation, and ultimately the Enlightenment.

Narinder and his wife Ravi: Fifty glorious years of married life . 1963 - 2013.

Karan, son of
Narinder and Ravi

Pia, daughter of
Narinder and Ravi

The Old is Dead, Long Live the New...

(Remembering 'The King is dead, long live The King!'... ha ha)

Drop the old, O self... drop the New

Free from both... beloved self...

Revel in the Old, enjoy the New...

Bowing at the Feet of the Guru... Dissolving in the Lord

Ever Free from "I", "Me" and "Mine"...

In the Nothingness of being, abide...

AUM

Can You Change Your Destiny?

The fates of souls are all by God ordained
According to the deeds that they have done.
That end that's destined ne'er to be attained
Will never be achieved by anyone
However hard they try. All those things, too
That are destined must occur one day,
Will come to pass whatever you may do
To interfere and try their course to stay,
And this is certain. At length we come to see
That it is best that we should silent be.
~ Maharishi Ramana

Can your Destiny be changed by you, Nari?

Dear narinder, HE who has written your Destiny can change it too, if HE be pleased... IF you can reach HIM.

And that happens when you Meditate. In the Moment of Enlightenment... the Sanchit Karma (Accumulated Storehouse of Karma) comes to an end.

The Prarabdha (Ordained for the present Lifetime), does not end, but becomes easier to bear. Pain is pain no more...

Meditation is the Way, therefore... Guided by an Enlightened Master, narinder, walk the Path... and erase the Destiny...

Accepting your ordained Prarabdha cheerfully, the account of the Previous Karma gets erased... and NO new Karma gets created. NOT accepting your ordained Prarabdha cheerfully, starts a new Karma, and a chain of Karma gets formed...

AUM

Am I?

Many Yugas before, I chose to enter a body, to share thoughts of Righteousness...

... And you people called me Krishna, the Guru of all Gurus... still remember me, worship me as Krishna...

And thousands of years passed... and I chose to enter a body again... to preach what Love is... and you called me Jesus! Even today, you continue to worship me as Jesus!

Another age... and I entered another body to give the self in you a message about Goftaan... and you called me Mohammed...

You never learn about the Truth of your own Being... but keep worshipping the Body I take birth in... when I entered yet another Body about 550 years ago in the Land of the Five rivers... you chose to call me Nanak...

Ah...

Very, very few are you, who can see that I am NOT the Body at all! The Body is born, and it dies one day... I am the Immortal One, who is the Light that illumines all the Existence... I am the Sun, the Moon, the Stars...

To those, who despair even after achieving name, fame and wealth... the Very World... I reveal my Self... I bestow on them the Gift of Meditation, and they come to realise that I am ever and ever their own self... we are NOT Two!!!

AUM

The True Guru is Only ONE

Aye... The true Guru is ONLY One... the One without a second... and HE it is, who has appeared in many, many forms including the great Ramana Maharishi...

And will continue to appear in many forms yet to come...

Ramana has been a spiritual Guide in narinder's Life too... along with Nisargadatta Maharaj...

BUT what awakened narinder to seek refuge in the words of all the Buddhas was the guidance of Sant Paranpal Singh Jee, and Mohinder Singh Jee... the Two outer Gurus that the Lord of all sent his way . .

AUM

FOR A MOMENT...

For a moment... narinder... is not concerned with "self, Self, God, Existence"...

FOR A MOMENT, narinder [WHO? God, Existence, Silence, Nothingness???]... is not concerned with "self, Self, God, Existence, Silence, Nothingness". He is concerned with...

He is concerned with the Being, who is in Pain, who is in Fear...

To him/her he says "Go to an Enlightened Master, ask him lovingly, trustingly, to help you transcend the qualities that are born of Prakriti (Nature), and which are the cause of your disturbance of Mind, your Pain, your suffering, your Fear, your delusion.

AND IF... you are unable to find/ recognise such a Master, pray to God to send you one... and help your Mind to recognise Him and trust Him."

Such a Prayer NEVER goes unanswered by the Lord.

AUM

The World has NOTHING to give to narinder

The five year old child in narinder's body was lured into the mysteries of titillation in childish sex by two older girls, one of them in her early teens... and the child's innocence was no more... it was replaced by a sense of Guilt, for what was being done was to stay hidden from the eyes of his mother and Others... this Guilt, followed by other different types of Guilt, was to trouble him for a long, long time... till Meditation came his way... Grace of God...

Time went on... childhood passed... marriage came, the world began to woo narinder-ness to its embrace...

Then came the Guru... in the early twenties.

At some point of time, in the Thirties perhaps, narinder realised that the World had NOTHING to give to narinder... and the Guru had much to give him... the Secret of Light... and Love... Love that does not wax and wane...

Meditation the Doing soon led to Meditation the happening... the Guru was smiling...

narinder also realised that he himself was the enemy of the Self. Choosing the Self, he decimated the self... and felt the Freedom from all pain and fear, angst and Guilt.. his face now shone with an ethereal aura... he was innocent again... like a child; childlike, but not childish...

narinder had become like his guru... he became the Guru...

Krishna, too, was smiling...

All this became Possible... only because, appalled by the sense of Guilt, narinder prayed to the Lord to send him a guru... and Krishna bestowed the Gift on him...

AUM

The Mysterious Ten Verses and One!

1. Of Brahman, did Brahman ask ... Lord, Teach me Brahman...
   To Brahman did Brahman say... "Son, You are Brahman!"

2. In Joy did Brahman receive... The Loving instruction of Brahman...
   With folded hands did Brahman again submit,
   "Lord... Lovingly, you bestow!
   But Brahman does not understand!"

3. To the humble Brahman did Brahman then instruct..
   "Your Humility, dear, is the doorway... My first Gift
   to you...
   Through this doorway, then, will you, one day,
   Receive the knowledge... The Knowledge of Brahman!"

4. Eyes raised to Brahman, the ocean watering the eyes with
   Love,
   Did Brahman, then ask again, "Gifts you bestow... there is
   no end.
   But the Gift that Brahman wants
   Is the gift of Your Self. Your own Self. The Self"

5. To the seeking Self, Lovingly did Brahman then bestow...
   The Great Gift of Vision. The Vision that is called
   Meditation.
   In this Meditation, did Brahman sit for Yugas
   For Yugas, did Brahman take asana... Yugas...

6. "Yugas" was only a word...
   Silence the Word's Being.
   And Lo! Time was No More,

What was, was... Only This Moment Now...

7. Yugas passed... and Brahman did smile on Brahman...
   And Brahman, opened the eyes. Then, to Brahman, spoke

8. "Lord, May I call you Krishna?...
   Krishna is the sound of Music that vibrates my soul!
   Lord, may I sing the song that thrills my Being,
   Krishna... Krishna! Jai jai Krishna!"

9. "Krishna! Krishna! Krishna indeed am I", Brahman smiled
   In Joy indeed, did Brahman smile!

10. And so!
    To Brahman did Brahman Bow!
    "Krishna... You are Brahman indeed!"

11. In Ten verses, Did Krishna sing...
    Sing of the Glory of Brahman!
    In Ten, did Brahman receive,
    Receive the Song of Krishna's Being!

The Ten were only One...
The One-ness of Silence of Being.
The Silence, which will Keep singing...
In Ten verses, the glory of Being!

"The teaching" said Brahman to Brahman... "Easy it is... This
teaching of Mine.
Easy as easy can Be! But to the non willing,
The teaching will ever remain
A Mystery... The Mystery of Being!"

AUM

Confirmation for the Enlightened:

One day, the earnest disciple got enlightened... and years passed...

He went to his Guru, bowed reverentially, and said

"I find it strange, Guru jee; we began with The Purpose of Life, its meanings... and now... I find that there is Neither any Purpose any more, nor any meaning for me... for all that is happening everywhere, and in everyone's Life, is ordained by God according to HIS immutable Law... Seeing all the upheavals and calamities occurring, I remain undisturbed... sometimes participation in activities takes place, sometimes I remain standing as a mere witness...

Actions, when they happen in me, are spontaneously according to the Teachings of the Scriptures...

Mostly persons around me call me a Sage... and sometimes, some call me a hypocrite... but what others say about me, does not disturb my equilibrium..."

"Yes", smiled the guru, "Blessed are you Nari... you have now reached the highest state of Being, after being enlightened... possibly, there may now be NO rebirth for you..."

Nari bowed to the Guru again, and touched his feet... and was dazzled by the Light that the Guru's Being was emanating.

The Guru at whose feet narinder was bowing, had left his body some eleven years before..

AUM

Purusha and Prakriti

In the beginning, there was only ONE,
the nameless one without the second.

He decided to become two, called Himself the Purusha.

Purusha created matter, and and filled Matter with a minute Portion of HIS BEING, and Life began.

And, THEN, the Purusha, filled Matter with Sentience, the Power to think, and human beings came into play.

To regulate the World of Beings, Purusha, created Prakriti, which manifested as the Three Gunas, Sattva, Rajas, and Tamas.

This regulation is through God's law... namely, 'what you sow, so shall you reap'... called in Science "Action and Reaction are equal and opposite."

NATURE, Prakriti, has NO mind of its own.

Nature is God's creation, His Law... inviolable Law... the Three Gunas that rule the world, according to HIS Law...

It is Purusha that has a Mind... the sentience of Beings.

And of course, it is Mind that, tired of the chaos and ups and downs, takes to Meditation, under Guidance of an Enlightened One... and evolves to its innate Purity... is able to remove its eclipsing by Ignorance.

Prakriti is often called 'Cheri' (Slave) of Purusha.

AUM

The Day has 24 Hours...

Each Hour a long 60 Minutes...

For 99.999% people, it is so very difficult for Time to pass... and they keep creating work to pass this time, work that often they are not in need of...

It is the Yogi who has mastered the Art of Doing NOTHING, when nothing is needed to be done... he relaxes, just lying down... often slipping into sleep (Yognidra)...

Doubly benefited is he... Doing nothing, just relaxing, he achieves the greatest possible... he gets liberated from the cycle of Birth and Death...
AUM

A Seed hidden in the Heart of an Apple...

*A seed hidden in the heart of an apple is an orchard
invisible. ~~Khalil Gibran*
To make it blossom, is required the Discipline of Meditation,
under the Guidance of an Awakened Master ~~ Narinder
A seed hidden in the heart of an apple is an orchard invisible.
Yes, as far as Plants and Fruit are concerned...

AS to Goodness, God and Truth, the seed is already present
within the self... and we can nurture it by surrendering to the
Guru, and following his Teachings.

To make it blossom, is required the Discipline of Meditation,
under the Guidance of an Awakened Master.
Without a Guru, it is very, very rare - though not
impossible! The Ego in oneself prevents one from listening to
the voice of God present as Breath and Consciousness in each
one of us.
AUM

How Many..."Ahas"... Ah?

How many... ahas... ah?

one in each lifetime
one in each breath
one in each joy of the song
one in each yearning and pain
one, and only one...

ONE

not knowing the One,
nari sought many
onc in cach lifetime
one in each breath
one in each joy of the song
one in each yearning and pain

but through the Grace of the ONE
one moment now
Nari was gathered by Him, the One
into His Embrace...

and then, narinder knew
knew beyond the sceptical monkey Mind

that

all were One

all are One
and
all that Nari was seeking
in each lifetime
in each breath
in each joy of the song
in each yearning and pain
was nought but The ONE!!!

and you are That!

you, you... and, YOU, you, Nari... you narinder...
you, my Friend
you are That
the 'I am' are you, Nari,
ah, narinder,
you, verily, are That!

ah, aha, aum!

AND Nari, Until the self is known,
until the ONE is known,
the seeking never stops,
the search never ends
and all is pain!

ah, aha, aum...
AUM

Ah Sweetheart, I will Always be There for You; Always!

NO! No, you will NOT be there for Me Always!

"There is NO such thing as Always", My Guru did say...
"There is ONLY This Moment Now...
Catch it in your Being, narinder...
And you have divined the Secret of Eternity!"

Things shall arise... only to vanish...

narinder is best served, IF he attaches himself nought to
Things, attitudes, concepts, yearnings, desires...
allowing them their fun and mirth, their Play... and
rejoicing now in their presence... only to rejoice in their
disappearance!

Enough, my Friend... if you are there for me NOW... just this
Moment NOW...
In Eternity, Love brooks no barriers... not in Life... nor in
Death it brooks a divide -
Love must sing its Song, when the Lover is willing to die!

Myriads are narinder's yearnings, each a pining for the Death
Divine
Innumerable the desires that on the Altar of Love, their souls
did sacrifice
and yet, another one did arise with its Song...
in the Beloved's Love to die!

Ah, sweetheart, I now know. I will NOT be there for you
Always!

AUM

Does the Mantra Given by the Guru ever Change?

The Answer came from the Inner Guru, one early morning at 2 AM.

The experience of many a time acquired a new intensity for the last hour or so... mergence with the Pranva, the silent sound of Aum... One-ness, in which totally totally the Mind, (Ego) became No Mind.

... A beatific experience of slow soft Blissfulness surrounding the Being, in which the body-consciousness completely disappeared... Only the Pranva remained... narinder was The Pranva, and the Pranva, narinder...

"Meditation is the ability to focus on a single Thought for a protracted period of Time, without any distraction"
~~ Krishnamacharya, great Sage.

Whatever be that Thought, also called the Mantra for Meditation, it ultimately becomes the Pranva... aummmmmmmmmmmmmm

AUM

MEDITATION

Meditation is the discovering of the Eternal in one's own self.

Few are able to achieve the promised results of Meditation: freedom from remorse, guilt, pain, fear and delusion; abidance in the Moment Now

What is meditation? Meditation is of the nature of Understanding. It is understanding of one's own being, one›s own self; understanding of one›s link with the rest of the Universe, of our source, of totality or whole-ness, of one-ness of the «I» in me and whatever the «I» can perceive or conceive.

It is the ability to direct the Mind exclusively towards an Object, and sustain that direction without any distractions.

Or . . .

It is the earnest Direction of the Mind exclusively towards an Object, and sustaining that Direction by refusing attention to its distractions.

The technique is learnt from an Enlightened Master. Books can only give you Intellectual Knowledge, and NOT the Wisdom of Realisation.

AUM

MORE ON MEDITATION

Meditate. Meditate. Meditate... Meditation is the Fountainhead of all Virtues...

All you read, all you write, all you do, will become a Blessing.

A Blessing to you... and a Blessing to Others who read your words.

Meditation... let us once again see what it is... and where it leads to...

It is the Effort of One, who is NOT yet established in the Awareness of ONE ALONE (THE ONE-ness)... to focus his Mind on a single Thought for a period of time (20 minutes? 30?), without any distraction... practising it at least once, and if possible twice a day...

This Practice brings about an ability in oneself to concentrate on whatever is being done, thus helping one to grasp more, the nature of the thing one is concentrating on... thus achieving more... achieving more leads to material well-being, which of course is very gratifying.

BUT, what is more beautiful... MEDITATION brings about a certain silent purification of thoughts... leading one to enquire about the Source of well-being and ill-being... virtue and vice... good and bad... and the why there-of...

Gradually it leads one to the realisation that the Source is ONE... and THAT One-ness, being ONE, is Nameless or is all

Names... and is The Doer and the Enjoyer... this brings about a tremendous silent feeling of Peacefulness.

In the beginning, it is not continuous... then, its duration keeps increasing... till ONE day, some day, while meditating there is an Explosion of that ONE-ness... the Light of lights, Consciousness... this is Enlightenment...

This Enlightenment then leads to greater and greater understanding of the words of Truth given in the Scriptures and to detachment from Maya (Materialism); this truth begins to get practised in action...

Then, there gradually happens the spontaneous renunciation of Sankalpa (self-will... conception or idea or notion formed in the heart or mind, solemn vow or determination to perform, desire, definite intention, volition or Will).

Ultimately there occurs a continuous, constant, 24-hour awareness of that ONE-ness or God... and abidance therein.

With Duality permanently dead, the Sage abides in the Self... a Blessing to the World, doing much GOOD to all around him... and leads others into THE SPIRITUAL PATH... AND ENLIGHTENMENT.

MEDITATION is best learnt under the Guidance of an Enlightened Master, or Guru.

"Egotistical involvement in Maya is filth; Maya is overflowing with filth. Under Guru's Instruction, the mind is made pure, and the tongue drinks in the subtle essence of the Lord.

The tongue drinks in the subtle essence of the Lord, and deep within, the heart is drenched with His Love, contemplating the True Word of the Shabad. Deep within, the well of the heart is overflowing with the Lord's Ambrosial Nectar; the water-carrier draws and drinks in the water of the Shabad.

One who is blessed with the Lord's Glance of Grace is attuned to the Truth; with his tongue, he chants the Lord's Name. O Nanak, those who are attuned to the Naam are immaculate. The others are full of the filth of egotism. || 2 ||"
~~ Nanak

AUM

The Nature of Meditation

Meditation, dear Seeker, is of the nature of thirst...

An inner yearning... a deep yearning...

to shed the false in 'narinder-ness'... and be naked;

totally naked... totally innocent like a child...

but

this innocence is something more than the innocence of a babe, whose innocence is the result of ignorance.

It is the innocence, the one side of the coin, the other side of which is Wisdom of experience of Life and living...

... the awareness of the Evil in birth, death, sickness, old age and pain... (Bhagvad Geeta, 13/ 9)

Today's Contemplation: [From: "Tsultrim Serri: Words for Dewa Chenpo 01 March 2010"]

What could be easier than resting?
Though you know, Dewa, the fallacy of that.
As the Buddha taught, "all pain comes from wanting"
Including wanting our thoughts to stop intruding on our practice
Our emotions on our life, and our desire for fruition on enlightenment.
Our wanting never stops until we see the truth, that's why resting is not easy.

We cannot learn to rest in what we are without help.
Only the great ones provide that help,
But where do we find them?
Many can give you the teachings, but who can give you the
experience?

AUM

Life and Death

Ah, narinder (Ego... or, Mind)

Have you not had your Fill of Sorrow yet...

That you still seek Pleasure!

Hollow are your tricks O mind,

No more Now shall narinder listen to Thee!

Die, die, O Mind... in your Death

Lies nari's Freedom from Pain

Die, narinder, die... die you MUST!

And, narinder...

Meditation is the Only... the only Way

AUM

Meditation Does not Happen?

"Nari?"

"Yes, narinder..."

"How, Why, and What?"

"What needed to be said, has been said, narinder. Now, Be Still, and Meditate."

"Nari?"

"Yes, narinder..."

"Stillness does not happen, Nari..."

"Then sprint, narinder... with all your might, run! Do not spare yourself!"

"Are you serious, nari?"

"Never more so. Run, as you have NEVER run before, and see!" (smile)

AUM

The Words of the Buddhas

The seeking of enlightenment is a concept troubling to the self... ah (Ego -self)!!!

The millions of words that Buddhas have spoken, narinder... who are they for?

And why millions of words, when just One Word is sufficient unto Love and God?

It is because... (and this is for the ego-self)... it is because words shall keep troubling the ego till the ego dissolves...

The ego's dissolution is a state wherein being troubled by concepts OR/ and efforts at realization, the concepts and conditionings of lifetimes just disappear for-ever... no concept, thereafter, is ever troublesome... in fact, all is so-o-o clear, that each word spoken by a Knower of Truth seems to be your word, your thought... your being...

And yet, take it from loving Nari, the path is NOT that simple, as the Mind would like it to be to be...

The Knowers' words have tried to convey what cannot be conveyed... and not just some words.

As long as you are on the path, you have not reached the Goal(Destination)... and when the Goal is reached, there is no path to traverse any the more... you are there... and you know it!

You know it... the self knows it for sure... and this knowing is not the Mind-created false knowing...

The blessed ones, like all my friends here including nari and narinder, keep walking this Path (this ever non-existing path-less Path), because...
... because the self is already That!
... and step by step, moving into Brahaman till the self is known HERENOW!!!

And then, NOTHING disturbs!!!

Words from the Enlightened Ones help us, encourage us, show us the way...

Each person has to be his/ her own friend... his/ her own counsel, his/ her own judge; and has to keep judging himself/ herself (not judging others)... and the judging is with regard to CONDUCT, his/ her own conduct...

When the self would truly be known, when 'Enlightenment' happens... nari would become aware that his conduct is totally (and Totally) in accordance with the conduct of the Buddhas... there is no difference at all!!!

Seeking now comes to an end; and now, the Nari-ness proclaims its budha-hood through words of love and joy to all...
... but each person, being what he/she is, receives from those words, only what he/she is ready to receive...

In a way, he/ she receives, just what is necessary for him/ her to move one step closer to Enlightenment...

And it just comes into Nari's awareness... that whatever he is writing here, is also equally applicable to him... it is applicable to all, this missive of Love... for all are the self... all friends here are highly advanced souls on the Path...

And, there is no competition on this path... there is no hurry to 'arrive'; nari-ness, when willing to die to nari-ness, moves ever so slowly into Death of nari-ness... and nari is no more, only the self is... pure, resplendent Light and Love, which embraces darkness of varied hues joyfully and lovingly...

As long as Time exists for nari... the past and future, more meaningful than the Present Moment of Herenow... nari has to keep treading...

Ah, once again so many words have got added to the millions that are constantly being shared... they are necessary, even though, no words are truly necessary!!!

When Light shall shine on itself... and sing its own song with Love and Joy... words shall cease... and, time too!

The Buddha's words "Yes, No, Both and Neither" will cease to trouble... in fact nothing will ever trouble the mind... the mind would have been transformed to No-Mind!!!

AND,

The Buddhas? Their complete message is One word... so simple, it's right before your eyes, but how very, very few ever see it. The word is "LOVE".

The seeking of enlightenment is a concept troubling to the self... ONLY to the Ego -self!!!

Ah, my friends, what more can Nari say, and how?

AUM

Yoganidra

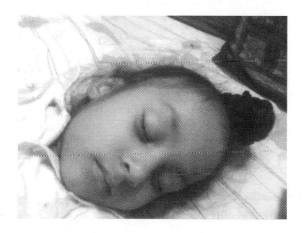

Before sleep, Meditate on God...

Meditation is to go into the silence of Desirelessness...

While in this Meditation, sleep will steal over you...

You will then enter Yoganidra... and your sleep will be very Sound and Peaceful.

AUM

Nirvikalpa Samadhi

The Highest possible Experince for a Human Being

The Highest experience of the sage is that of Nirvikalpa Samadhi... that of absolute all-pervading deathless Nothingness... wherein even the Thought 'I am' disappears... and with its disappearance, Time ceases to exist...

Then, at some point of Time, this Nirvikalpa Samadhi becomes Savikalpa Samadhi... the 'I am' arises as a thought... and along with it arises the Universe... and for long time the 'I-am-ness' experiences the One-ness of Consciousness, with many, many Universes seemingly floating in that Consciousness...

Then, in due course the Savikalpa Samadhi too comes to an end, as the sage enters the domain of Body-Consciousness, the Waking State. And then begin the day-to-day activities... the Sage's actions bathed in Righteousness...

These words get written just after entering that Waking State.

Willed and Directed by WHOM, do these words get written... and for whom, pray?

God gifts this experience of Samadhi to the sage at least once in every 24 hours... usually at Amritvela.

AUM

Ashtanga Yoga

Yogascittavrttinnirodhahah

The great South Indian Yogi, Krishnamacharya, who is no more, has translated the second Sutra of Ashtanga Yoga as: "Meditation is the ability to direct the Mind exclusively towards an Object, and sustain that direction without any distractions."

Ah, narinder, stop! There is nothing more to read... there is nothing more to know... there is nothing more to say...

Ah, my friends...

Words and more words light up the Song of Light...

More added every new day

Increasing the Words to awesome numbers... ah!

And only one poem, only one line

Is enough to de-eclipse the Sun from the dark cloud!!!

Ah, narinder...

Stop!!!

Begin, and Stop, just Stop!

There is nothing more to read...

There is nothing more to say....

Nothing more to know...

Nothing more to desist from 'knowing'... not-know!

Celebrate this Moment of freedom...

No ‹doing› any more, no ‹knowing› any the more!

Be purposeful, narinder...

Let the Goal be clear...

As clear as This Moment Now!

Let the step you stand on, itself become The Goal

Your Destination... Aum

And

Nari and narinder, pay heed to the words of wisdom

Uttered by the sages and seers of yore;

Let your movement into tomorrow, born of today,

Be one step closer to your Goal...

This Lifetime is precious,

Waste not a moment, waste not a day!

Meditate, meditate, meditate...

In Meditation, experience the Silence,

Silence, the death of nari-ness,

The death of narinder-ness... Aum

And, in that Death abide,

Abide as « Not- I»

Abide as "Not-self", Annatta

Nothingness...

And thus abiding,

Let the self guide the self unto the Light of the self for the sake of the self.

Die, nari, die; die narinder die...

Die and live forever and a day

The Deathless Life of This Moment Now...

AUM

What kind of Love are you talking about... Real Love?

"IF you are looking for Real Love, you've chosen the hardest task of all... the Work for which all other work is but preparation!"

Love does not mean 'surrendering'... losing yourself... it is a call to 'ripen'...

... don't look for straight lines, Nari... Life is never like that!

True Love is Death... a deep Discipline...

Discipline is a call to ripen... meticulous observance of the Discipline FREES you from the throes of Discipline... Meditation is the way.

Discipline remains no more a hardship thereafter! Thereafter is the Bliss of Sahaja... Spontaneity!

AUM

THE MISSIVE OF LOVE

Dear Friends,
Narinder writes this missive to you all with Love.
Let there be Joy in receiving, receive with Love.

A million words we keep reading, a million have been read
Examine your Mind's state, and right Now, find... become
aware...
That
That, for which the million words were read and heard, and
spoken too,
Is still far away; far, far away!
Do you think, then,
That reading a million more words, and hearing them, too,
You will find that
Which is not a Word; which, though the source of all words,
Is
Silence?
Not the word 'silence'
But
Silence itself.
Silence,
The beyond-ness, the transcendence, that which is the very
substratum of the Word
And Without which, no word will be intelligible!
And it would so seem
Truly seem
That we are up against The Impossible!
And yet, the Knowers of The Silence,
The Knowers of the Truth that is Silence of Being,
The Mother of all Creation and Creativity,

47

Have said:
Have said, that The Truth can be known,
Realised
As clearly as you can see the Palm of your own your hand!
AND
That Truth, that Reality of your own Self
Your own Being, is not...
Not your Body, mark you,
Not your Body, nor your Mind, nor your Intellect,
But that, which illumines your Intellect and your Mind,
And, your body enlivens, This Moment Now
That Truth
The Truth you seek
Is
Your own Self.
Your Own Self,
The 'I am-ness' needing no affirmation, nor ever suffering
denial of being.

When the Self is Known, All is Known,
Have the Knowers of Truth so affirmed!
And all knowers of The Truth have averred,
Have said,
That
No amount of Reading,
No amount of Reciting,
No amount of Hearing,
No Amount of Doing,
No Amount of Not-doing,
Will lead you into Silence of Being.
And yet Nothing is Irrelevant.
Make your Doing (Karma) a Yoga,
Transform your hearing Into Understanding,
Make your Recitation into 'The Way', The Japa Yoga,
Let your Reading to you become a Revealing

And
Realise the Self
That Leads you into Freedom from all Fear, All Pain, All
Doubts!
AND How???
Only One way, there is... The door is but One!
The Door is The Guru,
The Guru is the Door,
The Guru is the Dwara!
The Guru
Guru Means Light, True Light.
How can One, who has himself not known Light
Lead Darkness of Ego
Into Light that does not destroy the darkness, Ego
But Embraces it... to make it One with Light?

The Guru is ever in search of the Ego,
The darkness, which is ready to sacrifice itself,
In order to become Light.
Not become, exactly,
But
Discover that it is Itself the Light Divine.
Ever Free it is! And was always So!
And can never ever be Otherwise.
If You be That... My Friend,
You,
The One, who today is groping in darkness
And today, Here and Now, has understood the Essence of This
Missive
This Missive of Mine
Which is really not Mine... for it is The Eternal Missive for The
Seeking Hearts -
And narinder, one day, feeling that he had had enough of Life
and living

Life and Living, the worldly Way,
Had taken refuge in The Said Missive -
If you be The Friend,
The Seeking Heart,
Thirsty enough to Give up all elixirs but the Guru;
Then, who is The Guru
To refuse you entry
Into the Life Divine,
The Joy Eternal,
The Bliss Infinite Of The Moment Now.
This Moment Now!
BUT
Let me warn you,
Heed this Warning -
This Path is Not Easy;
It is Not for the Cowards, who are afraid of Death and Dying -
For The Guru
Will not have from you
Less than your Head.
With Love, My Friends, Nari began This Missive Divine
With Love, he ends... May all Joy indeed be yours,
Ever and ever.
May Krishna Bless you with Courage, Wisdom Strength and
good Cheer
This Moment Now.

AUM

Words can be Very Tiresome... ARE, in Fact!

narinder, too, went through this Tiredness... or, perhaps, is still going through it...

Ah, narinder!

This tiredness... Is it because, having posted some beautiful Thought (in the opinion of the self), one begins to wait for a response, that does NOT happen!?!

IF so, narinder, the reason of 'becoming tired' is within, NOT in the Words.

IF NOT, i.e. IF the Tiredness is NOT born of inadequate response, but is genuinely seeing the Futility of the Experience... all experience... well then, the Experience has served its Purpose. It has taken you beyond it!

In that case, both decisions... to withdraw from FB, OR stick to FB... would be correct... Your Heart can NEVER be wrong.

By staying on, narinder has 'nothing' to achieve... by leaving, he has nothing to lose...

AND/ OR conversely... By staying on, narinder has 'nothing' to LOSE... by leaving, he has nothing to ACHIEVE...

Aum

Yes, narinder?

Another aspect to help the intellect take seemingly a correct decision...

IF narinder... your stay with the Reading of Words, gives you a feeling of narinder-ness dying to itself... hastening the Death of Mind... stay on till the Death... do.

And IF... the Words Sojourn seems to perpetuate the narinder-ness... Well then, stay on... but be more mindful... Meditate. Meditate. Meditate. And make sure that your Experience with your Reading goes NOT waste. The Mind must be led to its death!

And... narinder... with a little help from the Lord... you CAN DO it!

Yes.

AUM

In the Throes of Corruption...

"When you see that in order to produce, you need permission from men who produce nothing - when you see that money is flowing to those who deal, not in goods, but favours - when you see that men get richer by graft and by pull than by work, and your laws don't protect you against them, but protect them against you - when you see corruption being rewarded and honesty becoming self-sacrifice - you may know that your society is doomed."

- Ayn Rand, Atlas Shrugged, 1957

In this present Movement of Time, Ayn Rand's words written in 1957 seem prophetic.

It is, verily, a doomed Society, where Values get eroded day by day...

It is only the Spiritualist who has some hope in the present Times... rising above the movement of Time...

Remains un-affected by the declining values...
and...
Is also able to raise hope in others around him.

Make your choice narinder... be with the world, or, be NOT-of-the- World.

And you Nari...
how did you manage it, Nari?

Manage what, narinder?

Surviving becoming a part of the prevalent Graft and the eroding Values...

It was simple really, narinder... with Dharma as my right Wing, and Karma, as the left Wing, i flew higher and higher into Nothingness, whenever any Graft became pleasing to the Mind... or even the values of the Society... and thus escaped all that.

AUM

PERENNIAL!

Was this written years ago?

A Moment comes in the Life of a Yogi when the Mind's labelling of Wrongs and Rights ceases to exist, there are just NO Wrongs and Rights... one begins to ACCEPT the Lord's Will and Law totally! THIS IS THE SURRENDER to the Lord that we keep talking about all the time...

When the intellect, the refined mind that has been curbed by Yoga (Meditation, and Spiritual Practices... like Satsang and Swadhyaya) also ceases to Be because it is absorbed in God; the worshipper perceives Him through his Self....
and abides with contented happiness in his own Self.

He apprehends God, but he dwells contented in his Soul...

In the moment of attainment he sees God,
face to face as it were,
but the very next moment he finds his own Self overflowing with the eternal glories of that God.

This is possible only if the stage of total surrender has been achieved.
And then:
"Be yourself... Love yourself... and BE!"
And if it is truly done:
Where does narinder exist?
Either with physical or subtle form of body?
No where... no more.

AUM

Patanjali's Yogasutra,
and Definitions of Meditation

Yogaschittavrittinirodha

The great South Indian Yogi, Krishnamacharya, who is no more, has translated the Sutra as "The ability to direct the Mind exclusively towards an Object, and sustain that direction without any distractions."

narinder meditated on the Sutra, and the following meanings arose from his being:

Yoga is the intensely thoughtful state of Thoughtlessness.

Yoga is the intuitive awareness of the River-bed beyond the flowing water in the Stream.

Yoga is surrender of the Mind to the Lord, the merging of the Mind in its Source.

Yoga is the Un-activity of the Mind.

Yoga is the denudation of the Forest that is Mind.

Yoga is the suicide of the self in the Light of the Self.

Yoga is the awareness of the eternal nature of the Present Moment.

Yoga is the obliteration of the Universe from the Mind in the cause of Self-love.

Yoga is the State of Grace, in which the tendencies of the Mind disappear.

Yoga is the practise of the detachment of Mind from its propensities by deliberately focussing it on the solitary desire for Reality of One's own self.

And... Yoga - as Practice - is the earnest Direction of the Mind exclusively towards an Object, and sustaining that Direction by refusing attention to its distractions.

All Gifts are from the ONE Source, God. It is the Lord's Gift, not subject to the Law of depletion, bestowed by the Lord on the earnest Seeker of Reality. He Himself receives that Gift by entering the Heart of the Seeker. [Ever present is HE in everyone's Heart, but the Seeker, NOW discovers that Presence].

AUM

ACCEPTANCE: The Gateway to Meditation

"When The Lord bestows on one, the Gift of Total acceptance of HIS Will... absolutely Total... then, one realises that "Ultimately NOTHING matters".

This is what my Guru, too, had said to me once, shortly before he left his mortal frame.

"You will realise, one day, narinder", he had said, "that, ultimately NOTHING matters."

It took me quite some time to realise that, even after my Enlightenment in 1982. BUT finally, i did. I understood that it is connected with Total Acceptance of God's Will.

Now, all around me, other people's conduct does not cause me to react as it once did. It elicits only a response from me... response bathed in Love and Compassion.

So does this Understanding enter the Minds of all who meditate, under the guidance of an enlightened Master.

AUM

O my Mind, Abandon Your Household Entanglements, says Nanak.

Does it mean, Nari, that you should leave home, go to a forest? Or, stay at Home... and stop taking interest in Household affairs, remain aloof?

Neither of them, narinder! What it means... is that you should stop expecting anything from the other members of the Household... Continue serving them as before... rather, even more consciously and skilfully, seeing God in them, BUT do not expect anything in return.

AUM

Each One of Us is Born with a certain Talent. This is our Seed Being.

1. Directly or indirectly, our Being shall try to express this Talent, to sprout, flower and come to fruition.
2. The world around us has its own urges its own Desires to fulfil.
3. There is a conflict. Our life is a conflict.
4. This very conflict becomes the Source of our growth, our ripening.
5. Existence, or God, the supreme Power, is our ONLY Friend, our supreme benefactor. The earlier we recognise it, the earlier we are able to tap our Potential, and the faster is our Progress in all fields, including the Material Field.
6. The Conscious 'tapping' of this Power is through Meditation.
7. Meditation flowers in us, through contact with the Awakened Ones. Through reading/ listening to their words. Through exposure to their physical aura.
8. Thus it was, that in ancient India, each family had a Kul-Guru, the family Guru, to whom each member of the Family bowed in reverence and obeyed. The sole Interest of the Guru was to help his disciple attain his Desires, to help him ripen, and lead him into Bliss that is not dependent on Objects, Relationships, or Achievements.
9. Thus it came to pass... that India became the Land of Dharma, Righteousness, the Way of achieving our highest Potential. Discovering this Bliss as our own inner Nature, became the Goal of Life for all Beings, rich or poor, male or female. Dharma became the Protector, the Guru.

10. And Dharma thundered!
    "Dharmo Rakshati Rakshitah"[Dharma protects those
    who protect Dharma]
    [Manusmṛti, Ch. 8, verse 15]

Dear narinder, will you protect Dharma, will you make the
study of Dharma a part of your Life and living?
AUM

When my heart overflows...

As it so often does
Your Gift to Nari...

When my heart overflows
The head, in reverence, looks around.
For a vessel, it looks around
To pour the Joy of Krishna-love abounding.

And often it is,
That it finds
No vessel waiting
No vessel willing!

Today, Beloved,
When the heart was full
Full and seeking
As the mother seeks the babe
When the breasts are full and overflowing
Bal- Govinda whispered into Nari's head...
"I am thy vessel, Mother,
Pour your bliss into me..."

And in the deep worship to thy lovingness,
O Krishna,
Nari bowed and dissolved into his Being.

AUM

TRUTH IS SIMPLE!

These words, Nari has written scores of times on many a
Forum, and then gone on to elaborate logically...

Scores of times has Nari written, and you have read...
Joyfully read and exclaimed "Aye. Aye, and Aye."

AND YET, see the Truth...
How many be the self... to whom NO Doubt remains after
reading the Post...
To whom, NO scepticism silently creeps in! Ah!

IF...
IF, you be ONE, blessed are you... ignorant NO More!
What are you doing here?
GO!

Go. Share the Truth with the Needy; with one in whom the
YEARNING for Truth has blossomed...
And, who is willing to pay...
The Supreme Price for the Truth, you are selling... Death of
Mind!

Go!
Go, Serve... for what higher Service, there be...
than helping a fellow human-being FREE the self from Fear,
Pain and Doubt!
So, the Upanishads did say... so the Sages extol!

AND...
IF scepticism still sings its silent song...
Meditate. Meditate. Meditate.
IF Meditation does not yet Blossom...
Strive to DO GOOD to others, surrendering the Fruit to the
Lord.

AND, if that too finds NO favour with the self, yet...
Seek the company of the Sages, and from their mouth,
Hear the words of the Lord, hear the Praises of the Lord...

THE CHANGING VICISSITUDES OF THE MIND, WHO CAN
TELL?
Ah, Friends... who?
Yesterday 's Moment was a moment Now
Today's Moment is a Moment NOW!
Tomorrow is waiting to enter as the Moment NOW.

BUT, the Beloved, NOW's Lord of Lords, smiles... and laughs...
As some narinder, to HIM, bows in Joy...
No, narinder... it is NOT for You to think and Analyse the
Mystery of the Dream in the Reality of NOW

that for you, shall always remain...
Nought but a Dream.

"BUT, all IS Well... nor can it ever NOT-Be so..."
Sings Loud and Clear! The Song of the Now.

So Friends... bear with narinder...

The Invitation to Nari's Page shall remain the Eternal Song...
Come, weary Traveller... come, and sip a word...
rest a while... and resume your Journey...
Let narinder's Page be The INN... ever available, with Open
Doors!

AUM

All Songs are Songs of Love

Singing "I love you... please accept my Love... reject it not...
And Return my Love... i pray"

But Human Beings, being only human, sometimes reject your
Love... and return it not...

But when you sing the Song to the Lord... you sing for HIM...
Never does he reject your Love... but returns it manifold
multiplied... the Bliss of HIS love you cannot bear any More!

AUM

You are Supreme, My Friend. AYE!

O narinder,

You are Supreme... AYE... all around you, persons come (arise in your Consciousness?)... persons disappear... events happen... sentiments arise... emotions flower...thinking happens... EACH a moment's guest with the self you are... just a moment's guest... ah!

With YOU, ever with you... ever, and ever, with you... the only companion, the only friend, and perhaps the enemy too (LOL)... is YOU!

AYE! You are YOU... You are Supreme...

Who can hurt you BUT You?

Love yourself. Love is a feeling, not a thought! Feel your self.

Love yourself. Anything that is NO JOY to you... anything that could lead to feelings of negativity... DROP it! This is the Meaning of "Love Yourself".

BE STILL, narinder, and feel the wordless Silence say silently "I AM"... I am Supreme.

Yes Nari... now, i understand!

ACTUALLY, my Friends... there is NO nari, NO narinder... Ha ha ha!

narinder, who can hardly ever do RIGHT exists not, even as Nari, so pious that he can do NO Wrong, is but a Thought... waves in the Ocean called Nothingness... (smile)

Nari and narinder... narinder and Nari sing their Duet... seeking an Entry into the Heart of the Seekers of Truth, as understanding of Conduct that liberates the self from the throes and woes of the March of Time, which happens to be Adharma!

The Beloved keeps smiling ♥

... To go beyond the Illusion... to be FREE from the Illusion of duality... is the highest (so-called) achievement of human Intellect!

Freedom from the self!

Becoming FREE from the self... the Self remains ever free from right and wrong, sin and virtue... Satyam, Shivam, Sundaram, it is... the very epitome of Truth, Goodness (Beneficence), Beauty...

Infinity taken away from Infinity... the Infinite still remains the Infinite! Bliss, that embraces all duality... ♥

Aye, Nari and narinder exist not... nor do they exist-not! LOL

AUM

Oneness of God, Unity of Mankind: The Quran Sharif

narinder's AIM in writing this is to show that All Religions emanate from the Great One-ness, and the Quran says that all the Scriptures are to be trusted as The Word of God...

Oneness of God, Unity of Mankind: The Quran

There shall be no coercion in matters of faith. -- 2:256

Say (O Muhammad): «We believe in Allah, and in what has been revealed to us and what was revealed to Abraham, Ismail, Isaac, Jacob, and the Tribes, and in (the Books) given to Moses, Jesus, and the Prophets, from their Lord: We make no distinction between one and another among them, and to Allah do we bow our will (in Islam).» -- 3:84

For each we have appointed a divine law and traced out the way. Had Allah willed He could have made you one community. But that He may try you by that which He hath given you He made you as ye are. So vie one with another in good works. Unto Allah ye will all return, and will then inform you of that wherein ye differ. -- 5:48

Do not dispute with the people of the Book [Jews, Christians, Sabeans], unless it be in a way that is better, save with such of them as do wrong; and say: We believe in that which has been revealed unto us, and revealed unto you; our God and your God is One, and unto Him we surrender. -- 29:46

O mankind! We created you from a single soul, male and female, and made you into nations and tribes, so that you may come to know one another. Truly, the most honored of you in God's sight is the greatest of you in piety. God is All-Knowing, All-Aware. -- 49:13

Allah is He, than Whom there is no other god;- Who knows (all things) both secret and open; He, Most Gracious, Most Merciful. Allah is He, than Whom there is no other god;- the Sovereign, the Holy One, the Source of Peace (and Perfection), the Guardian of Faith, the Preserver of Safety, the Exalted in Might, the Irresistible, the justly Proud. Glory to Allah! (High is He) above the partners they attribute to Him. He is Allah, the Creator, the Originator, the Fashioner. To Him belong the Most Beautiful Names: whatever is in the heavens and on earth, doth declare His Praises and Glory: and He is the Exalted in Might, the Wise. -- 59:22, 23, 24

FURTHER:

To know the Truth for yourself, all the Knowers have suggested Meditation is the Way. In the Silence of Meditation, one becomes ONE with God...and hence, becomes a Knower of the Self... what he IS!

Meditate, my Friend, and Know for yourself!

Allah is all for DOING GOOD DEEDS and singing the Praises of God; an essential step towards pleasing Allah.

Teachings of all Religions (Knowers) are to be accepted as TRUE... says Quran Sharif. I quote once again:

Say (O Muhammad): "We believe in Allah, and in what has been revealed to us and what was revealed to Abraham, Ismail, Isaac,

Jacob, and the Tribes, and in (the Books) given to Moses, Jesus, and the Prophets, from their Lord: We make no distinction between one and another among them, and to Allah do we bow our will (in Islam)." -- 3:84

AMEEN

Loving Remembrance of GOD
Should be Continuous...

In Indian Culture, Loving Remembrance of GOD should be continuous... it keeps the Mind from its negative propensities.

AUM,(Amen, Ameen) is the symbol for that loving remembrance... the utterance of aum, before beginning any Undertaking, invokes God's Blessings... and utterance of aum after the DOING is finished... wards of the effect of any lapse on the part of the Mind that may have crept in unintentionally... SO SAY THE SAGES...

The next logical doubt that may arise is, why NOT utter it silently, in your mind? After all, Religion, truly speaking, is a very private affair... a very valid doubt, this!

Why does narinder then, use this symbol in all his writings? narinder is unable to answer it...

Perhaps, it is an arising from the Inner Being... as are all the arisings in us from the same Source... [The Source is ONE... the all-pervading Energy called GOD/ Existence]... and the purpose of Existence may be to spread this knowledge to others, through narinder... NOW, just see... my constant Use of the Word aum has made you ask this Question... and as a result, you are reading this answer.

Knowledge of Truth, and remembrance of God will enter many who may read this... thus making their Lives peaceful and harmonious.

It is possible, that Loving Remembrance of God may also become your Way of Life, albeit silently in your mind... LOL!

SECOND:
Ultimately... this Silent sound, uttered silently, in the Mind... becomes the GREAT MANTRA for Union with GOD. Samadhi. Self realisation.
What is Meditation? Focussing your Mind on loving Remembrance of God, for a protracted period of Time, without any distraction.

While teaching Meditation, a Word (Mantra) is given by the Guru to the Sishya (disciple) to utter silently, as a loving remembrance of GOD. Whatever mantra is used... as we move deeper into Meditation, Consciousness changes it silently and ULTIMATELY, to this silent sound... mmmmmmmmmm... hastening our Realisation.

AUM

Misunderstanding, Dear Friend, is the Creed of the Time...

The Yogi's touchstone is the self... he (she included) watches his own self... his own response/ reaction to the situation...

His own response/ reaction to the situation, he watches... and finding disturbance in his own self... he 'knows' he needs to walk the Discipline of Yoga, even more earnestly... ♥

AUM

What does 'Remain Dead While Yet Alive' Mean?

"I have searched and searched, but I have found no way to remain here; so, remain dead while yet alive." ~ Nanak

Nari, what does 'remain dead while yet alive' mean? Tell me once again...

Death of the body, everyone sees, narinder... but the Sage is able to see what does NOT die, when the body dies.

'Remaining dead while yet alive' means... becoming aware of that Truth. That happens when the Ignorant mind dies. The Thinking process drops...

AUM

THE SYSTEMS IN THE BODY:
Have YOU ever wondered about them?

"The beings born of eggs, born of the womb, born of the earth and born of sweat, all are created by You. I have seen one glory of Yours, that You are pervading and permeating in all." ~ *Nanak.*

Ah, narinder... often is Nari amazed at HIS Creation above... and the Systems in each body, where there is a body (and perhaps, even if the Body is not perceptible to human eyes)... The systems, the Digestive, the Circulatory, the Reproductive, the Respiratory, the Skeletal, and the Nervous system... [In human beings the Nervous system blessed with Sentience, the Power of Thinking...and Intelligence].

Have YOU ever wondered about them, narinder?

Meditate on it narinder, and discover the Secrets - and the Mystery - of the Gross, the Subtle and the Causal Bodies.

Then, go beyond the Systems, to abide in the Bliss of Fullness that is the great Void... Bliss and Love that are your own true Nature...

AUM

The Travails of an Aging Body:
The Mind's link with it... the Viciousness of the Movement of Time!

Aum... dear one, what narinder is now going to say here, very few may understand... but YOU definitely shall....

All our 'knowing', intellectual or Realised, is worth it ONLY IF it can bear Fruit in the present Moment...yes!

We are aware of the negative and diabolical March of Time... so ordained by None Other than Him, who was benign in the Satyuga, the Age of Virtue and Truth...

In the Present times, the Imperfections of Scientific Belief and experimentation (in spite of all the progress in Science and Technology), and the vicious Greed of the Drug Mafia (medical or otherwise - LOL), play merry hell into humanity.

narinder looks at his own body, 75, with its imperfections due to the aging process, and/ or the medicines/ drugs that entered the body because of so-called medication...

This Moment Now, firmly ensconced in the KNOWLEDGE of the Supreme's Law, and understanding that **ALL (ALL - Good or Bad - all!) is part of HIS Law and dictates**... narinder abides in the Bliss that embrace both the Good and the Bad in the body's present state.

All is Well. All is Good. All is just as it should be. The Present Health or Ill-Health, The reduced Vision in the One Eye, and the Good Vision of the other eye. It could also have been that both eyes may have lost their Vision! narinder rejoices in the gifts of the Lord. He rejoices even in the bad vision of one eye. **It is Meditation that has been the greatest help.**

narinder has been off drugs (allopathic medicines) for a very long time; he takes only Ayurveda Herbal Drugs. They have their roots in ancient Loving-Research of the rishis/ sages. Meditation, a little exercise, a little self-control in diet, are very Good Caretakers of the aging body.

narinder has been able to lead a reasonably healthy Life in body and mind... and is confident of continuing to do so till the body systems fail on some excuse or the other, as they must some day!

The World may call these Understandings madness, foolishness... BUT... he calls it The Beloved's Blessing... narinder lives in Peace, and shall leave the body in Peaceful-ness, carrying it into the next Birth... with yet greater joy and Love of the Lord.

Apply all this, my Friend, to your own body's state of health, the Mind's state of evolution and experience of HIS Grace.

A Moment comes in the Life of a Yogi... when the Mind's labelling of Wrongs and Rights ceases to exist, there are just NO Wrongs and Rights... one begins to ACCEPT the Lord's Will and Law totally! THIS IS THE SURRENDER to the Lord that we keep talking about all the time.

At the end of the Day, we only have our own Mind/ Intellect as the instruments of Play...

So...

Be yourself... Love yourself... and BE!

AUM

Macrocosm and Microcosm

Macrocosm and Microcosm are two words.

Macrocosm means... from the point of View of the Whole... In this Post from the Point of View of God.

Microcosm is "From the Point of view of the miniscule"... in this Post, from the Point of view of Man.

From the point of View of the Whole, God... Earth, when seen, would appear like a very, very small, still dot...

From the point of view of Man (Microcosm)... there is such a great Movement going on...Ocean liners plying in the Ocean... on the Ocean liners, so much movement going on... Airplanes flying, To and Fro, from one corner of the earth to the Other...

NOW THINK ABOUT IT... From the Point of View of GOD... wherein Earth itself is a dot, is there any Movement at all? Will it NOT seem total STILL-ness? And the Great Planetary Movements... even they are NOT visible at all! There is NOTHING but Silence, void, Nothing-ness!

An Enlightened Sage can perceive this Stillness... He can see from the Point of View of the Macrocosm... TOTAL STILL-ness... NO Movement at all anywhere!... even as he can see from the Microcosm, much activity in the universe.

Thus he sees, just as Nanak says "Na kuchh hoa, na kuchh hog" [Nothing ever did happen... nor is ever happening]

The Sage keeps singing "Jo hua howat so jane, Karne har aap pehchane" [The Enlightened One knows, what has happened... he also knows the Doer... God is ever and ever the only Doer]

He knows whatever happens will happen, according to God's law... All is Just and Fair... thus, there is Nothing ever to fear...

He says that although much seems to be happening... in Reality, Nothing ever IS!

"Na kuchh hoa, na kuchh hog"

AUM

I am the Vastness

I am the vastness

Vaster than vastness;

I am also the minitude

minuter than minitude;

I am the un-knowable.

Love from nameless Nari to you O joyful and loving Friend,

who are yearning for truth,

pining for the un-knowable,

and crying in love for the divine within your own soul...

And,

the pain of the sorrow of not-knowing yourself

that blossoms as yearning in your being!

The fulfilment, too you are

of the love that silently abides in the heart for the self,

for yourself,

the self ever known as 'I am'

that brooks no separation

even when you say, 'not-I', 'not-I'.

And with the two wings of knowing and not-knowing

you can fly, and fly, and keep flying

to destinations un-known, and not-knowable!!!

Meditation has given the Gift to narinder;

Now he can see, and for once, he understands, Being within himself.

He understands the meaning of Freedom. Be within your Self. Be at peace with your Self. Be your Self.

He understands it now.

He grasps it now.

Ah, my Friend! Be Love. Be Light. Be the I Am. Be within. And most of all, know you can fly, without being a slave to the idea of wings.

AUM

I Know but Little, my Lord...

ALTHOUGH the Sage has realised his One-ness with God...
and abides in the declarations of the Mahavakyas... 'Ayam
Prajanam Brahaman', [I myself am Consciousness that is
Brahaman]...and, 'Ayam Atma Brahaman '[I am the deathless
Being that is Brahaman]... going on to 'Aham Brahamasmi'
[I myself am Brahaman or God]...

Yet he also realises, and says 'Meri Mat Thoree, Ram' ~
Nanak' [My Understanding is not Vast... it is but Little, O
Lord]... 'aape jane aap' [Only YOU know your own Self and
YOUR Vastness].

On the one hand, the sage is God... yet... he is humble
enough to know his smallness... just as the Particle of the
Himalayas can say 'I am the Himalaya'... yet it remains but a
particle... the minutest part of the great Himalayas.

AUM

ENLIGHTENMENT

Lying close to the Beloved, whether it be the Spouse, the Sibling, the Parent, the Child, Guru or God, bodies touching, just touching OR, not touching... just Love flowing...

If touching, the sense of who is touching whom is lost... boundaries cease to exist... manifestation seems to merge into non-manifestation... no boundaries... happening and non-happening merging... flowing into each other... no boundaries...

Moments pass... is it minutes... or hours... or just ONE moment... Time has ceases to exist...

What more can narinder say... what more can he know... both Knowledge and Ignorance have disappeared...

Such are the Moments of Union with the Lord, Govind-milan...

Back to the ordained Play of the Day, after this Blissful Union with the beloved Lord... life continues...

The Sage lives as is a witness to this Life of his... seeing with wonder, the Perfection of HIS Creation... total Perfection of HIS drama... No Imperfection... NO complaint.

AUM

The Enlightened Being

Attributes of an Enlightened being: His Understanding and Conduct

These are posted for the Mumukshus, who feel that they have finally realised the Self; to judge themselves, and NOT others.

He knows that The Lord God totally pervades everywhere and permeates all beings.

It is God, who plays being the Ignorant.

It is God, who plays being the Seeker.

It is God, who plays being the Guru.

The God-conscious being looks upon all alike, like the wind, which blows equally upon the king and the poor beggar.

To the God-conscious being, friend and foe are the same.

The God-conscious being is steeped in humility.

The God conscious being knows that he is neither the Doer, nor the Enjoyer.

The God-conscious being is neither attached to, nor pursues Material Goals any longer.

The God-conscious being shows kindness to all.

The God-conscious being delights in doing good to others.

The Suffering for most majority is on account of penury in Material wealth. The God-conscious being is an out and a out Giver. He gives to all, who come to him in need. He never refuses those who are in need. He becomes a conduit of God.

The God-conscious being is the Giver of the way of liberation of the soul.

Says the Holy Book::

The Saints are tolerant and good-natured; friends and enemies are the same to them. O Nanak, it is all the same to them, whether someone offers them all sorts of foods, or slanders them, or draws weapons to kill them. || 27 ||

They pay no attention to dishonour or disrespect. They are not bothered by gossip; the miseries of the world do not touch them. Those who join the Saadh Sangat, the Company of the Holy, and chant the Name of the Lord of the Universe - O Nanak, those mortals abide in peace. || 28 ||

Many have reached the total Intellectual Understanding of the above... but they should know that this intellectual Understanding has to become their CONDUCT in Action.

AUM

Enlightenment and Subtle Ego

Nari?

Yes, narinder?

Methinks... They, who are enlightened... the Gurus, are most in need of examining themselves for their subtle Egos...

Yes, narinder... That is why i had once posted the following words of Maitreya:

SPIRITUAL EGO:

The spiritual ego is subtle, cunning superior, inferior and secretive.

The spiritual ego develops because ego has to live somewhere until it dissolves.

If you are a seeker of truth, the ego identifies with your quest and can become serious and secretly superior.

The inner reality of seekers is never quite as beautiful as the ideals of their tradition and they decorate their ego so it looks a little nicer. This is a common trap for many seekers and one from which it is difficult to escape.

Authenticity and playfulness are the antidote. for this you will need support from those who are already living in this way.

When the ideal is authenticity, not purity, you are free to be yourself. authenticity and playfulness give you the space to face yourself as you are and to confront your darkness consciously. This conscious self-encounter brings purity indirectly, without the hypocritical burden of a spiritually pure ego.

What is meant by "authenticity and playfulness are the antidote"? It is SILENCE alone that brings the understanding of the un-knowable (by the intellect/ mind).

Ah! To feel the Bliss and Beauty of This Note, my friends, Meditate. Meditate. Meditate. For this you will need support from those who are already living in this way.

Aum

Yes, narinder?

Thank you, Nari.

AUM

This is for Many, Many Naris and narinders:

Read the Penultimate Truth below once again O Nari... O narinder:

We all need Direction, from Time to Time... till we are Enlightened.

Then we teach Others... lead them unto Enlightenment. ♥

When this world had not yet appeared in any form, who then committed sins and performed good deeds?

When the Lord Himself was in Profound Samaadhi, then against whom were hate and jealousy directed?

When there was no colour or shape to be seen, then who experienced joy and sorrow?

When the Supreme Lord Himself was Himself All-in-all, then where was emotional attachment, and who had doubts?

He Himself has staged His own drama; O Nanak, there is no other Creator. || 1 ||

When there was only God the Master, then who was called bound or liberated?

When there was only the Lord, Unfathomable and Infinite, then who entered hell, and who entered heaven?

When God was without attributes, in absolute poise, then where was mind and where was matter - where was Shiva and Shakti?

When He held His Own Light unto Himself, then who was fearless, and who was afraid?

He Himself is the Performer in His own plays; O Nanak, the Lord Master is Unfathomable and Infinite. || 2 ||

When the Immortal Lord was seated at ease, then where was birth, death and dissolution?

When there was only God, the Perfect Creator, then who was afraid of death?

When there was only the One Lord, unmanifest and incomprehensible, then who was called to account by the recording scribes of the conscious and the subconscious?

When there was only the Immaculate, Incomprehensible, Unfathomable Master, then who was emancipated, and who was held in bondage?

He Himself, in and of Himself, is the most wonderful. O Nanak, He Himself created His Own Form. || 3 ||

When there was only the Immaculate Being, the Lord of beings, there was no filth, so what was there to be washed clean?

When there was only the Pure, Formless Lord in Nirvaanaa, then who was honoured, and who was dishonoured?

When there was only the Form of the Lord of the Universe, then who was tainted by fraud and sin?

When the Embodiment of Light was immersed in His Own Light, then who was hungry, and who was satisfied?

He is the Cause of causes, the Creator Lord. O Nanak, the Creator is beyond calculation. || 4 ||

When His Glory was contained within Himself, then who was mother, father, friend, child or sibling?

When all power and wisdom was latent within Him, then where were the Vedas and the scriptures, and who was there to read them?

When He kept Himself, All-in-all, unto His Own Heart, then who considered omens to be good or bad?

When He Himself was lofty, and He Himself was near at hand, then who was called master, and who was called disciple?

We are wonder-struck at the wondrous wonder of the Lord. O Nanak, He alone knows His own state. || 5 ||

When the Undeceiveable, Impenetrable, Inscrutable One was self-absorbed, then who was swayed by Maya?

When He paid homage to Himself, then the three qualities were not prevailing.

When there was only the One, the One and Only Lord God, then who was not anxious, and who felt anxiety?

When He Himself was satisfied with Himself, then who spoke and who listened?

He is vast and infinite, the highest of the high. O Nanak, He alone can reach Himself. || 6 ||

When He Himself fashioned the visible world of the creation, he made the world subject to the three dispositions.

Sin and virtue then began to be spoken of. Some have gone to hell, and some yearn for paradise.

Worldly snares and entanglements of Maya, egotism, attachment, doubt and loads of fear; pain and pleasure, honour and dishonour - these came to be described in various ways.

He Himself creates and beholds His own drama. He winds up the drama, and then, O Nanak, He alone remains. || 7 ||

Wherever the Eternal Lord's devotee is, He Himself is there. He unfolds the expanse of His creation for the glory of His Saint.

He Himself is the Master of both worlds. His Praise is to Himself alone.

He Himself performs and plays His amusements and games. He Himself enjoys pleasures, and yet He is unaffected and untouched.

He attaches whomever He pleases to His Name. He causes whomever He pleases to play in His play.

He is beyond calculation, beyond measure, uncountable and unfathomable. As You inspire him to speak, O Lord, so does servant Nanak speak. || 8 || 21 ||

AUM

Pain, Fear and Delusion: The Cause

This body beautiful, and the feeling that you are that body, is the cause of all your Pains, Fears and Delusion.

And the Realisation that you are NOT the body, but THAT Breath and Consciousness which vitalizes the body, and illumines the Mind in the Three states of Consciousness (Waking state, Dream state, and Deep-sleep state), liberates you from the Three.

Very, very difficult it is to drop the Body-consciousness. It happens only when God, in HIS Grace, makes available to you an Enlightened Master, who has realised his ONE-ness with God.

Grace alights in many ways... God it is, who sends it...

AUM

Drop all Judgement

Concern yourself with the Truth you seek.

Some friends bring to narinder some ugly facets of some sage or the other...

Yes, controversies do get raised... i am aware...

My Guru said to me one fine day "Drop all judgement, narinder, and concern yourself with the Truth you seek."

One of the most satisfying feelings that narinder has lived with for many years now... IS... that Meditation, God, and Guru has become the Truth of CONDUCT for narinder... spontaneous and easily expressed.

narinder stopped judging... and Wow! What a Joy it is!

ALL Sages are... for narinder... GOD in human form...

... Just like you too are... or, narinder also is... and it is GOD's Will that various sages bestowed on narinder-ness and his wife.... some very divine Moments in Timelessness...

... In other words, they contributed to narinder dissolving in Timelessness... Yes, THEY could only be God!

You are welcome...O FRIEND... to be true to yourself... to express your Beliefs and Being as you feel... narinder appreciates it... you are you... God playing YOU, as God so wills...

narinder is NOT offended when he hears you express your views about the Sages...

Yes... Some of them become controversial... BUT... who is narinder to judge them? narinder, who does not even know himself!!!

This Moment sharing with you is a Blessing... Thank you, my Friend, who is reading this...

AUM

The Knowledge of Enlightenment

Can an enlightened person know that she/he is enlightened? And if so, does she/he claim it?

Yes. When he gets Enlightened, which is the Gift of God, he KNOWS!!!

ONLY he can know it... whether he is enlightened or not yet enlightened, and he needs to continue his sadhna even more earnestly. NO-ONE else, but him.

And all the Sages have said so... it is not their Claim (Claim has an element of Ego). It is just their statement.

Kabir said so. So did Raheem. So did Namdev. So did Nanak, So also all Sages...

More recently, Osho and Nisargadatta Maharaj also said the same.

They said "The Lord, in HIS Grace has bestowed enlightenment on us, and Now HIS Light also shines through us."

And yet, it may happen, that the Egoistic mind may cheat the Seeker, posing to be enlightened.

To avoid this there is a need for the True Seeker, to be very, very watchful. He needs to see whether sankalpas still keep arising in him, and what kind are they, especially whether his Mind is still pursuing Material Goals.

AUM

Be a Watcher!

Be a Watcher.

Become aware that your True Nature is just 'Watching'.

Witness Consciousness is what you were, you are, and shall ever be...

The Doer is ONE... the ONE without the Second... the all-pervading, beginning-less, unborn, self-supporting, UN-knowable Spirit...

You are NOT the Doer... only The Watcher are you.

AUM

Love: The Highest Blessing

"Love is what you want... and Love is what you shall get", said narinder's Guru to him.

Every time narinder would meet and part from the Guru, he would ask him to give narinder his love. [1961 to 1974]

Then it happened sometime in 1974 that:

One day his Guru asked narinder to drop him from his house [in Jhansi], which he was visiting, to the City in his [narinder's] car.

On the way, at very secluded place in Company Bagh, he suddenly asked narinder to stop; and alighted from the car.

Narinder touched his feet and said "Pitajee (Father... all his devotees addressed him thus), please shower your Love on me."

His guru became expansive...
"What kind of a person are you Bhandari jee... that you keep asking me always for Love.

Some ask me for success in examinations, or Business. Some others ask me for the Gift of well being of the body or that of near and dear ones. Numerous other gifts people keep asking me for... but very, very, very Few ask for Love..."

"Go! I give you Love."

"You need not get up early in the Morning to do your Sadhna... you need not now go through all the Steps that one has to go through to get Liberation."

"When God asks you why you did not do so... tell HIM that Pitajee said so."

As a result of this Gift from Pitaji... so many Lifetimes of Sadhna have been cut short.

God, then, sent to narinder his next Guru, who introduced him to formal Meditation. [1977] and continued to guide narinder, till narinder received from the Guru and God, the Gift of Enlightenment [Jul 1982]

Nari went to meet Pitajee in Jhansi again in April 2000. And Pitajee gave him the Ultimate Gift: "I bestow on you all that I have", he said.

A month later, he shed his mortal coil.

Pitajee's last blessing has led to Nari's Consciousness to rise every year from the then present level to a yet higher level... Newer and newer vistas of the Knowledge of Truth are becoming his experience. He feels that this Lifetime of his may possibly be his last Lifetime.

While I cannot cut short the Sadhna [as my Guru did], of those of my Disciples who have Faith in me and ask me to give them Love... I bestow my Blessings... to hasten their Sadhna. ♥

AUM

Body, Mind, Intellect

The physical body, the densest aspect of the human personality, contains the five organs of perception and the five organs of action. The size and shape of the body differ from individual to individual, but the essential material composing it and the functions of the organs are common to all. Again, the subtlest aspect, the Consciousness, which is the core of man's composite personality, is one and same in all human beings. The variable factor in man is the mind and intellect equipment. The mind is the seat of impulses and feelings, and it is common to all living creatures. Animals also possess a mind, but man alone has the capacity to discriminate and analyze his feelings as and when they arise. He alone can allow his actions to be guided and directed by his power of discrimination instead of being driven and carried away by momentary impulses and feelings. This faculty of discrimination, this power of judgment, this capacity to discern what is to be done and what is to be avoided, is the function of the intellect. The kaleidoscopic patterns of experience are, therefore, attributed to the difference in texture and quality of the mind and intellect. In fact, it is only the mind and intellect equipment which come in contact with one another whenever there is a meeting or transaction between two individuals.

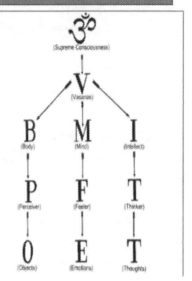

Body, Mind and Intelligence

For the Seekers, an important Read. Especially the Exercise to go into the Beyond...

These words below of Swami Chinmayananda describe the Truth of the Body, Mind and Intellect very Beautifully:

Self is: Breath, Movement, Consciousness. The three are Life. Breath and Movement only,(or Breath sans movement and consciousness), no-Consciousness is Coma.

Self is: Body, Mind and Intelligence.

Self is: Perceiver, Feeler and Thinker.

Self is: Objects, Emotions and Thoughts.

Body is related to Perception, and Objects. Mind to Feeling and Emotions. Intelligence to Thinking and Thoughts (analysis, judgments)

~~ Swami Chinmayananda.

And the exercise below, says Nari, has the potential to lead the Seeker into the Yonder beyond... into the Truth of his Being.

Perform this exercise, daily after your Meditation. DO IT again, again and again. One day, there will be an Explosion... Enlightenment. The Purpose of your Life would have been achieved. You will become a Blessing to the World.

The Whole vast Universe of myriads of Objects can be reduced to just Five; a Sound, a Touch, a Form, a Taste, a Smell. These FIVE can further be reduced to One: a Thought. Each is a Thought.

What now remains is Two; the Thought and the Thinker.

BUT the Thinker is himself a Thought in the self (Mind). The Thinker and the Thought are ONE. The Vast Universe is thus ONE, just a Thought in the Thinker. When the One-ness of the Thinker is perceived, there is Silence. The Universe ceases to exist. Shoonyatta. Nothingness.

This Nothingness is the Experience of a Sage. He withdraws his senses into the self through Meditation. The Universe and the self cease to exist. Neither Universe nor he exists in Reality. Neither He, nor the Universe, nor God.

And Now... He allows himself to become the senses... the five senses. And each sense to express itself in myriads of Thoughts. AND LO! within a fraction of a second, in the NOW (for there is NO such thing as Time in Reality), a whole Universe comes into Being... becomes REAL!!! (Wonder of Wonders)!!!

~ narinder

... This exercise came to narinder from the Satguru.

AUM

Self is Breath and Consciousness

Just Breath, and Consciousness...
A great Sage has said:
Self is: Breath, Movement, Consciousness. The three are Life.
Breath and Movement only, (or Breath sans movement and
consciousness), no-Consciousness is Coma.

Read these words again.

Is the word 'movement' required there?

No, it is NOT. It is redundant. Self is Breath and
Consciousness. Just Breath, and Consciousness. Movement
need not be there.

As a matter of fact, it is Stillness that leads to Samadhi.

A great Lesson for all. Read watchfully. Do everything
WATCHFULLY.

Watchfulness is the attribute of your own True Nature,
which is Sat-chit-ananda (Truth, consciousness, bliss) that
lies eclipsed by Ignorance till it is de-eclipsed through
Meditation.

AUM

Birth and Death exist in Duality

The Human Being experiences Highs and Lows in duality...
pleasure and pain, honour and dishonour, riches and
penury, praise and censure...

One day, becoming aware of the suffering that all these
cause, one prays to God for Freedom from Duality.

God, then, sends to one, the Guru; and the Seeker, walking
the Path under his Guidance, meditates on the Formless
immaculate God.

And, one day, happens the Enlightenment, that Freedom that
he sought.

When Duality existed, so did the Non-duality.

BUT, when Duality ceased to exist, so did Non-duality.

The State of Mind of such a Sage cannot be put in words. He
spends the remaining days of his ordained Life, living in
Duality, bathed in the aura of non-duality.

It is said that it takes four more Births to end the cycle of Re-
incarnation, but these Births are free from the sufferings
of duality. In these Births, the Sage becomes an instrument
of God, teaching others the Way to self Realisation or
Immortality.

AUM

My Friend, You Make Me Smile... Yes...

Smile is always the Beloved's own Expression, and Gift...

narinder dissolves in Gratitude...

Ah!

All Gifts are the Beloved 's gifts...

So that narinder can meditate... and dissolve in Gratitude.

Gratitude is the Way to the Beloved's heart. The Beloved's own Gift...

And finally, ONLY the Beloved remains... Just the Lord... THE ONE...

The One without the Second...

Thank you Lord...

aum

When you meditate on the Lord, you attain a certain Balance.

Buddha has given the Name "Samyak" to this spontaneous Balance. The Centre Point of all opposites... where there is TOTAL STILL-ness, and which is the starting point of dual expression in either direction.

The Lord of all expression, in HIS Creation of insentient Nature, abides in every atom as that Centre... that Balance... that Still-ness... Perhaps, that is the Secret of Nature's magnificence and beauty!

And then... the Lord creates HIS Masterpiece... the Sentient Being... and for HIS own Joy eclipses that Centre (HIMSELF)... HIS own Play... HIS own Leela... so that HE, HIMSELF, can play as the Human Being (you?)... play at discovering the Secret of His own Source!

Ah, narinder... you are yourself the Light that you are seeking... Be Still... regain your Balance... the Centre... the Beloved ever smiling... the Lord ever Joyous in Play...

If the Universe can make the tiny beautiful snowflake so complex yet balanced, think what YOU can do when in synchronicity with the Universe! Just a thought...

Ah, narinder...

YOU CAN DO IT!

Be Still and Know THAT I AM. Be Samyak. Be the Balance.

Meditate. Meditate. Meditate.

AUM

When it is Time for a Near
and Dear One to Depart

A day comes, when a person has to see his/ her dear ones leave this world... it is God's Gift that a person leaves... or, else more and more suffering would ensue...

What one can do is to... serve ones near one with so much love, that... that it makes the last moments easier to bear. Love has that magic...

... At the same time, remain detached... serving becomes easy and pleasurable, when detached.

By becoming detached, on does oneself the greatest favour possible... as this enables him/ her to move into the Beyond yonder... and gradually become enlightened, to merge in the Lord.

AUM

Some Gems from Kabir

(Kabir is one of medieval India's greatest sages; his spiritual verse is widespread on its own and also quoted in the Sikh scriptures).

Even if you do not see the Path, do not run away; this is the highest wisdom. He painted the great picture of the world. Forget this picture, and remember the Painter. This wondrous painting is now the problem. Forget this picture and focus your consciousness on the Painter.

I searched the whole world for Him, but I found Him near myself. Within myself.

That cheater, who cheated and devoured the whole world - I have cheated that cheater, and my mind is now at peace.

Only the mind can deal with the mind; says Kabir, I have not met anything like the mind. This mind is Shakti; this mind is Shiva. This mind is the life of the five elements. When this mind is channelled, and guided to enlightenment, it dies to itself, and discovers the secrets of the three worlds.

The fifty-two letters have been joined together. But people cannot recognize the One Word of God.

Through these fifty-two letters, the three worlds and all things are described. These letters shall perish; they cannot describe the Imperishable Lord. || 1 ||

Wherever there is speech, there are letters. Where there is no speech, there, the mind rests on nothing. He is in both speech and silence. No one can know Him as He is. || 2 ||

If I come to know the Lord, what can I say; what good does it do to speak? He is contained in the seed of the banyan-tree, and yet, His expanse spreads across the three worlds. || 3 ||

One who knows the Lord understands His mystery, and bit by bit, the mystery disappears. Turning away from the world, one's mind is pierced through with this mystery, and one obtains the Indestructible, Impenetrable Lord. || 4 ||

The Muslim knows the Muslim way of life; the Hindu knows the Vedas and Puraanas. To instruct their minds, people ought to study some sort of spiritual wisdom. || 5 ||

I know only the One, the Universal Creator, the Primal Being. I do not believe in anyone whom the Lord writes and erases. If someone knows the One, the Universal Creator, he shall not perish, since he knows Him. || 6 ||

Kabir speaks the Shabad, the Word of Truth. One who is a Pandit, a religious scholar, must remain fearless. It is the business of the scholarly person to join letters. The spiritual person contemplates the essence of reality. According to the wisdom within the mind, says Kabir, so does one come to understand.

The Holy Book contains many Verses of Kabir.

The above are taken from Kabeer's Bawan Akhree (the Fifty Two letters of Gurmukhi script), Pages 340 to 343 in the Holy Book.)

"All the Scriptures contain words and words of the Lord. Forget the words, but catch the Writer, the Lord" ~ narinder

AUM

Be the Breeze...

Are YOU that Breeze, O beloved zephyr, whose eyes happen to alight on these words?

All that the scriptures speak of, all that the Sages declare... IS... for narinder... ONLY for narinder...

The Bible was written for narinder,

The Bhagvada Geetha too,

The holy Quran, too, is for Nari...

If freedom from narinder-ness he seeks!

All that narinder writes...each word!... all that narinder writes is for the Breeze willing to become pregnant with the fragrance of Truth...

Are YOU that Breeze?

Does the Breeze of Love enter your Heart... or do you allow it to pass by, never touching you?

AUM

All is Beautiful.
That is all I Can Say.

Nari, in the last few days, i have been having very many strange spiritual experiences. Though quite blissful, i am bewildered and confused. I also feel somewhat intimidated. Can you guide me? ~ narinder.

Dear narinder, I have read all your words about the various experiences happening to you.

The answer is very simple... very short too...

Let come, what comes. Let go, what goes.

All is well... All is beautiful. That is all I can say.

This is valid also for all the Experiences yet to come. Just as the Moment NOW is fleeting... so is every experience.

In this sense... NOTHING is happening.

The feelings of intimidation are caused by your Mind, which is dying, and feels threatened. Let it die to the self. It is a Gift from God.

Go through the various writings in this series, read as many as you can daily.

You are getting the Call from the Beyond... Is it not beautiful?

AUM

SILENCE is What You Are...

YOU are the Word... and YOU are the Great all-pervading Silence, from which the Word arises and dissolves in.

Understanding thus, says narinder, Nari becomes silent and abides in THAT Silence.

Verily, only YOU know YOUR-self... and make available THAT Knowledge, to Your devotees, who worship YOU in Love.

AUM

Silence, the Womb of the Word

The awareness of Being, just Being 'I am ', silent awareness...
wherefrom is it arising? Is the Source not Silence itself... and
'I' is just a word... and Silence and the word 'I' are ONE.

I am... THAT silence. Some may call it the self...

The Game of the self is for the self.

The understanding that spurs the self to go beyond words...
and becomes the Realisation that the self in ALL is the same
silent awareness... And is the Self that persons call GOD.

The Understanding... the gift of the Guru and God...

From the Silence, then arise, words bathed in the fragrance of
Silence.

Knowing this Silence, one enters one's ALONE-NESS... in that
Alone-ness, arises Love... that one shares LOVE with all...
truly with all.

Alone-ness... Silence... Love... are ONE.

But, the Mind is a cheat...

It produces lack of Confidence in the self... as also
scepticism... by attaching the self to the False...

BUT Truth conquers all... and ONE day... Silence begins to
sing its song... the Song of the Self... the Song of Alone-ness
that is Love...

AUM

NO Thoughts to Live By

Shortest, sweetest, most satisfying is the Silence that, while giving approval to all analysis and experiences, ITSELF remains nought but SILENCE.

Abiding in the silence, leading all unto silence, the Sages and the Knowers have spoken also for those who wish Silence (and creation of silence) explained... and Wow! How many words they have left as heritage!

narinder finds his Joy in just THAT Silence. Meditating on the formless being.

There is great joy in dissolving in the Lord's promise below:

"Fix your mind on Me; be devoted to Me, sacrifice to Me, bow down to Me; having thus united your (whole) Self with Me, taking Me as the Supreme Goal, you shall come to Me" ~ *Bhagvad. Geeta Ch. 9/34*

And then, the sole Joy of expression... (for the days' 24 hours call for 'action' and 'doing')... becomes... either speaking of the Beloved, OR, hearing the praise of the Beloved...

The Beloved says:

"I am the Source of All; from Me, everything evolves; understanding thus, the Wise, endowed with loving Consciousness, worship Me."

"With their minds wholly resting in Me, with their senses absorbed in Me, enlightening one another, and ever speaking of Me, they remain satisfied and delighted." ~ Bhagvad. Geeta Ch, 19/ 8-9.

GREETINGS and GOOD WISHES:

May This Moment Now, flowering as the next 24 hours, enable us to go beyond the words that enslave us to the Mind.

May the year to come bestow on us words that liberate us from the tyranny of Words...

AUM

So Said the Sage Namdev jee:

One stone is lovingly decorated, while another stone is walked upon. If one is a god, then the other must also be a god. Understanding this, says Naam Dev, I serve the ONE Lord.

IF, God is in my Heart... HE must also be in the Other's Heart. Understanding this, i serve the One True Lord, says narinder.

AUM

The Roses Said...

Roses said to narinder "We are Givers... we allow all to bask in our Fragrance... each one, may he be a saint or a sinner... we love all".

Now narinder understands why everyone loves roses...

AUM

Walking the Path of Love that YOU are!

The New Day bought narinder a Message...

Ah, narinder... NO doubt, I am NEW!

BUT... Do not lose yourself in my Newness... for, there is Nothing New under the Sun.

What has been will be again, what has been done will be done again; there is nothing new under the sun. ~ ~ *Ecclesiastes 1:9*

And narinder, thrilled, began walking... Walking the Path of Love...

QUO VADIS (Where goest thou), narinder?, he suddenly heard his inner Voice say

Be childlike, Yes!... but... be Not a child, narinder!

The Wisdom of Lifetimes lived in Disciplines that FREE you from all disciplines... has sacrificed itself to make you childlike...

Be thou childlike narinder, yet be NOT a child, nor childish!

And then spoke, narinder's Heart...

A Rose... a Rose...

A Rose again for you, narinder

A white Rose... The white Rose, this time...

A White Rose... signifying Purity and Love

For you, who are Love...

You, who love the Rose... and love too, the Thorn

From Joy to yet greater Joy, God is guiding you, narinder...

From Love to yet greater Love

From Light to yet subtler Light of Being... ah!

For you . . my Friend... this white Rose...

THE White Rose, Dear narinder...

who, having understood that

This Lifetime is given to us by the Beloved

for the Purification of the self

Choose to walk the Path of Love,

and Love's Discipline!

AUM

Nau-nidh (Nine Treasures of Wealth)

This article will focus on what are the ਨਉਨਿਧਿ (Nau-nidh) or 'nine treasures of wealth'. This term is mentioned in the Ardaas (recited daily by Sikhs) and in Gurbani. Sri Guru Gobind Singh Ji, the Tenth Guru, writes the first part of Ardaas.

Guru Ji ends this verse by writing:
ਤੇਗ ਬਹਾਦਰ ਸਿਮਰਿਐ, ਘਰ ਨਉਨਿਧਿ ਆਵੈ ਧਾਇ॥ ਸਭ ਥਾਈਂ ਹੋਇ ਸਹਾਇ॥

Remember and meditate upon (Guru) Teg Bahadur; and then nine sources of wealth will come hastening to your home. (O Respected Gurus!) kindly help us everywhere.

'Nau Nidh' (Punjabi ਨਉ ਨਿਧਿ) appears in Sri Guru Granth Sahib 45 times.
Nine Worldly Treasures.

Nau Nidh includes:
1. Nine Worldly Treasures
2. Nine Spiritual Treasures

In the context of Gurbani the Nau-Nidh or nine sources of wealth are related to 'Naam' (the Lord's Name).

THE NINE WORLDLY TREASURES:

According to Indian thought traditionally Nau Nidheeaa(n) or Nine treasures are described as the following:
'Padam Nidhi' - Attainment of children, grand children, precious metals, gold, silver, and the like

'**Mahaan Padam**' - One gets Diamond, Rubies and other precious stones. gems, jewels etc

'**Sankh**' - delicious things to eat

'**Makar**' - training in the use of arms and Rule over others

'**Kachhap**' - clothes, food grains, corn and the like

'**Kund**' - dealings in gold

'**Neel**' - trading in precious stones, gems and jewels

'**Mukand**' - mastery of the fine arts, Music & Poetry

'**Kharab**' or 'Warch' - riches of all kinds.

THE NINE SPIRITUAL TREASURES:

Bharosa - faith. A deep Faith in, and Dependence on, God. The firm Faith in Waheguru is the first and foremost experience of a practitioner of Naam.

Leenta - An absolute attachment to (absorption in) God.

Santokh - Contentment, Detachment - From Family, Friends & Worldly Possessions.

Hukam - Acceptance of and Total Surrender to the will of God.

Sehaj - Equilibrium and Equipoise of the mind.

Anand - Perpetual delight and Permanent joy.

Vismaad - Ecstasy: Joy plus wonderment, forgetting the self.

Nadar - An awakened soul considers God as the prime reason of his attainments and that his own efforts means nothing. The attitude keeps ego far away from the person.

AUM

An 'Open and Shut' Case

This is an 'Open and Shut' case:

I shut my eyes. Watching happens, Nari seeing...

1. Darkness that seems more of Light than Darkness.
2. Hearing the Soft, Silent continuous humming of AUMMMMMM...
3. Sees some words arise in him, urging him to write about it... and...
4. Sees the Deed done...

The above words get written... each click of his finger in the Momentary NOW.

The above becoming a 'Whole' message having a Meaning... a message that shall remain in the Pages of a book, even though the event has passed long ago...

Hence do the Histories get written and read... the Writer, if he is a Yogi... moving into the Unconcerned NOW... oblivious of what was written, what is being read... and what Effect it shall have... the future events that may unfold... the Wars that may get fought, the elusive Peace that shall get sought by all...

All Seeking, all Thirst, all adding to the Thirst endlessly... co-creators in the Drama... that has been written, produced, directed and acted by Existence, for its own Leela, for its own Joy...

Wow, narinder, WOWW!?!

Yes, Nari, yes!

AUM

The Mumukshu

A Mumukshu is the one who is intensely yearning
for Liberation from these cycles of birth and death.
Mumukshutva is a power that gives strength to develop
Vairagya (dispassion) and Bhava Virakti (detachment).

What does a Mumukshu do?

The mumukshu is inspired by an inner urge to acquire
knowledge of the following:

I. Tattva Trayam viz.,
    i.   The Real (Tattvam)
    ii. The Means (Hitham) and
    iii. The End or Objective (PurushArtham)

II. The relationship between the three eternal entities viz.,
    i.   The Sentient self (Chethana and the chetan mind)
    ii. The Insentient matter (Achetan, and the achetan mind)
    iii. The All-sentient (Iswara)

Acquisition of the knowledge of the above is called JnAnam.
Mere acquisition of knowledge (JnAnam) is not enough.
It should be reflected in appropriate conduct (AnushTAnam).

HOW DOES THE MUMUKSHU ACQUIRE THIS KNOWLEDGE?
The mumukshu will seek a Qualified preceptor (AchArya),
take refuge at his feet and beseech him to impart the
required knowledge.

AUM

FOR THE MUMUKSHU:

WHAT IS THE RELATIONSHIP BETWEEN CONSCIOUSNESS AND ENERGY?

Modern physics has discovered one of the greatest things ever discovered; and that is: matter is energy. That is the greatest contribution of Albert Einstein to humanity: $E = mc^2$: matter is energy.

Matter only appears; otherwise there is no such thing as matter. Nothing is solid. Even the solid rock is a pulsating energy, even the solid rock is as much energy as the roaring ocean. The waves that are arising in the solid rock cannot be seen because they are very subtle, but the rock is waving, pulsating, breathing; it is alive.

Friedrich Nietzsche has declared that God is dead. God is not dead; on the contrary, what has happened is that matter is dead. Matter has been found not to exist at all. This insight into matter brings modern physics very close to mysticism, very close. For the first time the scientist and the mystic are coming very close, almost holding hands.

Eddington, one of the greatest scientists of this age, has said, "We used to think that matter is a thing; now it is no more so. Matter is more like a thought than like a thing."

Existence is energy. Science has discovered that the observed is energy, the object is energy. Down through the ages, at least for five thousand years, it has been known that the other polarities - the subject, the observer, consciousness - are all energy.

Your body is energy, your mind is energy, your soul is energy. Then what is the difference between these three? The difference is only of a different rhythm, different wavelengths, that's all. The body is gross - energy functioning in a gross way, in a visible way.

Mind is a little more subtle, but still not too subtle; because you can close your eyes and you can see the thoughts moving, they can be seen. They are not as visible as your body; your body is visible to everybody else, it is publicly visible. Your thoughts are privately visible. Nobody else can see your thoughts; only you can see them - or people who have worked very deeply into seeing thoughts. But ordinarily they are not visible to others.

And the third, the ultimate layer inside you, is that of consciousness. It is not even visible to you. It cannot be reduced to an object, it remains the subject.

If all these three energies function in harmony, you are healthy and whole. If these energies don't function in harmony and accord you are ill, unhealthy; you are no more whole. And to be whole is to be holy. The effort that we are making here is to help you so that your body, your mind, your consciousness, can all dance in one rhythm, in a togetherness, in a deep harmony - not in conflict at all, but in cooperation. The moment your body, mind and consciousness function together, you have become the trinity, and in that experience is the divine.

You ask, "Please say something about the relationship of consciousness and energy." Your question is significant.

There is no relationship of consciousness and energy.

Consciousness is energy, the purest energy. The mind is not so pure; the body is still less pure. The body is much too mixed, and the mind is also not totally pure. Consciousness is totally pure energy. But you can know this consciousness only if you make a cosmos out of the three, and not a chaos.

People are living in chaos. Their bodies say one thing, their bodies want to go in one direction; their minds are completely oblivious of the body - because for centuries you have been taught that you are not the body. For centuries you have been told that the body is your enemy, that you have to fight with it, that you have to destroy it, that the body is sin.

Because of all these ideas - silly and stupid they are, harmful and poisonous they are, but they have been taught for so long that they have become part of your collective mind, they are there - you don't experience your body in a rhythmic dance with yourself.

Hence my insistence on dancing and music, because it is only in dance that you will feel that your body, your mind and you are functioning together. And the joy is infinite when all these function together; the richness is great.

Consciousness is the highest form of energy. And when all these three energies function together, the fourth arrives. The fourth is always present when these three function together. When these three function in an organic unity, the fourth is always there; the fourth is nothing but that organic unity.

In the East, we have called that fourth simply the fourth - turiya; we have not given it any name. The three have names, the fourth is nameless. To know the fourth is to know the divine. Let us say it in this way: the divine is when you are an organic orgasmic unity. The divine is not when you are a chaos, a disunity, a conflict. When you are a house divided against yourself there is no divinity.

When you are tremendously happy with yourself, happy as you are, blissful as you are, grateful as you are, and all your energies are dancing together; when you are an orchestra of all your energies, the divine is. That feeling of total unity is what the divine is. The divine is not a person somewhere, The divine is the experience of the three falling in such unity that the fourth arises. And the fourth is more than the sum total of the parts.

If you dissect a painting, you will find the canvas and the colours, but the painting is not simply the sum total of the canvas and the colours; it is something more. That "something more" is expressed through the painting, the colour, the canvas, the artist, but that "something more" is the beauty. Dissect the rose flower, and you will find all the chemicals and things it is constituted of, but the beauty will disappear. It was not just the sum total of the parts, it was more.

The whole is more than the sum total of the parts. It expresses itself through the parts but it is more. To understand that it is more is to understand the divine. The divine is that more, that plus. It is not a question of theology; it cannot be decided by logical argumentation. You have to feel beauty, you have to feel music, you have to feel dance. And ultimately you have to feel the dance in your body, mind and, soul. You have to learn how to play on these three energies so that they all become an orchestra. Then the divine is - not that you see it; there is nothing to be seen. The divine is the ultimate seer, it is witnessing.

Learn to melt your body, mind, soul. Find ways in which you can function as a unity.

The above words are Osho's. And who is Osho? In the Ultimate Truth Osho is not a body, nor Mind, Nor Intellect... is pure Consciousness... is NO-word... is Silence... is Void... is Non-existence... is Energy, just Energy...

This One-ness or experience of Oshoness... of Being... is experienced by the Sage in Nirvikalpa Samadhi... and cannot be described in words...

NO pictures or Images can be taken or made of the Experience.

In this Experience, all Questions drop off...

ONLY a Human Being, through Spiritual Discipline and Meditation can experience the above.

Benefit of This? Freedom from Pain, Fear and Delusion; and Abidance forever and ever in deathless Bliss and Love, expressing them in Action...and spreading them around oneself.

One perchance in Thousands walks the Path... and one, perchance amongst thousands who walk the Path, reaches that Experience...

One in a Million...

It could be you... yes... it could be YOU...

AUM

Yet More for the Mumukshu

There are many forms or ways of meditation that erase one's personhood (Ego)... it gets incorporated throughout one's day... erase, erase, erase.

YET, until the Truth of Being - the ONE-ness of the Deathless Nameless Creator of ALL Creation - is realised, whereby these ways become available to Mind, MEDITATION, deeper and deeper on the Naam, leading to the continuous hearing of the hum of the Silent Sound of AUM, the Anhad Naad... IS THE WAY...

With the Explosion of ONE-ness in Nirvikalpa Samadhi, The Mind (Ego) dies forever...

One in a million realises this Truth... and sings the Praises of the Guru and THE GOD.

The key of the Guru opens the lock of attachment, in the house of the mind, under the roof of the body. O Nanak, without the Guru, the door of the mind cannot be opened. No one else holds the key in hand. ~~ Nanak

AUM

(Aummmmmmmmmmmm, the TRUE NAAM)

The Beloved's Grace is Guiding You, Dear Mumukshu

It is your own Good Sowings of the Past, that are bearing Fruits of Longing and Love for the Lord in you...

And, your present Love and Longing for the Beloved, invoke HIS Grace.

The chain of cause and effect, as HIS Valid Law, is leading the self towards the Death of all residue of negativity sown in the Past many lives... this is it that is called Death of Mind... Death of the Mind's attachment to the Body and the senses, which becomes the Root of all evil.

One day, this Discipline, whose main constituents are Remembrance of the Lord in Love, Doing Good Deeds, Meditation, Prayer and Gratitude (~ Nanak)... liberates the self from all Discipline...

The Mind having become the Divine Mind (the Krishna/ Christ Mind), now effortlessly adheres to the Five constituents above in Action, in Conduct... No formal Discipline is now needed. The Seeker has become the Sought.

You have become the Buddha Mind... THE BUDDHA!

Not only has the self now been redeemed... but the Buddha Mind redeems all its ancestors, and keeps sowing Seeds of Spirituality in seven generations to come...

And, all who come in contact with the Buddha Mind...

The "I, I, I" of I AM has now become the Silence of "Not-I, Not-I, Not-I".

So, say the Scriptures, the Sages and the Saints.

Smile, narinder, smile... The Lord is your Guide!

AUM

Narada's Bhakti Sutras

Dear Friend... Narada's Bhakti Sutras was one of the Four Books that nainder's guru, Air Commodore Mohinder Singh, gave him... and which helped narinder to move into self-realization!

Withdrawal from One's duties...

Narada's Bhakti Sutras, the ancient treatise on devotional Worship tell us... that gradually, the Bhakta, in his alignment with God, withdraws from all Duties towards the world... he has NO self-Will.

ONE duty that is binding even on the Bhakta, who has died to the self (ego), IS... his Duty towards his own body... he shall look after the body's needs (not the Mind's dictates) till his last Breath.

Look after your body, Dear Friends... allow there to be a balance in all your activities... eat sufficiently, sleep adequately... balance your Exertions with adequate recreation, which is not heavy on the body or the Mind.

In Bhagvad Geeta, the Beloved Lord says: [Ch. 6/16]

Verily, YOGA is not possible for him who eats too much, nor for him who does not eat at all; nor for him who sleeps too much, nor for him who is (always) awake, O Arjuna

Each event calls for our action on TWO fronts:
1. Towards the world... and
2. Towards oneself.

And both, too, are linked... ACTUALLY, each response/
reaction of the self, sooner or later, ends up with the Reaping
by the self...

Blessed is the response that leads the self one step closer
to Death of the self... to LIBERATION, which really means...
Freedom from Pain, Fear and Delusion, in this very lifetime!

AUM

Shatter the Illusion of Time

Will you meet yourself AGAIN, narinder?

Can you remember your face, what it looked like a hundred years before your father was born?

The meeting is always in the Now... will always be in the now... NEVER in some foreseeable Future of Thoughts!

And that Meeting 'happens', ONLY IF THE ILLUSION OF TIME IS OVER... when you have died to the self, while still alive.

When you have died to the self, you will be able to remember your Face... what it looked like a hundred years before your father was born!

AUM

narinder Was Dreaming....

Nari was enjoying himself at a Disco, when he heard his Cell-phone ring...

But he could not hear narinder's voice...

narinder, he said, speak louder... or better still, ring me after an hour. I cannot hear you in all this din at the Disco!"

YET, Nari could clearly hear the resonance of the Silent Sound of Aum... the Anhad Naad... embracing softly the truly loud noise at the Disco...

Sound louder than that which is presently going on drowns the softer sound... YET, NO sound, however loud, can drown the humming of the Anhad Naad.

The Anhad Naad is the supreme purifier of the Body and the Mind of the Yogi.

Aummmmmmmmmmmmmmmm

AUM

narinder Was Dreaming Again

All around him was Light, which illumined the Objects...
which enabled the Eyes to see...

Became aware that This Light was illumined by the Light of
Consciousness, which enabled his senses to function in their
respective fields... enabled him to see the Light that illumined
the Objects... which enabled his ears to hear...

And this Consciousness was itself resounding
deathlessly as the Silent Sound of aum...
mmmmmmmmmmmmmmmmmm... was God.

This Light was called God... was God. Consciousness
was God.

When Wakefulness happened to narinder at 5 am... all
around him was dark... and the Light of Consciousness was
illumining the Darkness...

And this Consciousness was itself resounding
deathlessly as the Silent Sound of aum...
mmmmmmmmmmmmmmmmmm... was God.

AUM

Once Again, Was narinder Dreaming

narinder was dreaming: he was on board a train, moving in its ultimate speed towards Howrah... he also became aware that behind this train were moving various kinds of traffic, all moving with their ultimate efficiency...

Suddenly the train slowed down... and so had to, all the traffic moving... slower and slower... and yet slower... till the train stopped... perhaps just a couple of hours short of Howrah... very galling it was to all... all who were travelling in the train.

So also very galling to the vast traffic behind, which too, had to stop...

And then, the train started moving again... faster and faster... and was almost at the Howrah station, or very near it... and narinder became aware that Howrah was his room...

Was it his room? ...Because he became aware that the Train had started moving again... faster and faster... at last it did move into Howrah... and Howrah was the Constant and continuous hum of the silent Resonance being heard in his inner ears... This Resonance was the ultimate station... he had arrived... the ultimate destination had been reached...

His eyes opened... narinder was in his room.
But the feeling that he had reached the ultimate
Destination, which is the Resonance, humming of
aummmmmmmmmmmmmmmmmmmmmm...

This feeling now remains... it is now 2.40 AM (Clock Time)... and he abides in this Resonance... the ultimate deathless expression of the One without the Second... and he is ensconced in this feeling... and he is aware that this will always remain... In the domain, where there is NO Time, it will remain...

The ordained life of the body/ mind/ intellect complex called narinder is being lived out, while the nameless being in narinder and the Resonance remain, each the other...

Free is narinder from all worries, pain, angst, fear, past and future... he abides in eternal Peacefulness... teaching others how to move into THIS Peacefulness...

Opened the Holy Book, which said:

The True Guru has listened to my prayer. All my affairs have been resolved. Deep within my mind and body, I meditate on God. The Perfect Guru has dispelled all my fears. || 1 ||

The All-powerful Divine Guru is the Greatest of all. Serving Him, I obtain all comforts. || Pause ||

Everything is done by Him. No one can erase His Eternal Decree. The Supreme Lord God, the Transcendent Lord, is incomparably beautiful. The Guru is the Image of Fulfilment, the Embodiment of the Lord. || 2 ||

The Name of the Lord abides deep within him. Wherever he looks, he sees the Wisdom of God. His mind is totally enlightened and illuminated. Within that person, the Supreme Lord God abides. || 3 ||

I humbly bow to that Guru forever. I am forever a sacrifice to that Guru. I wash the feet of the Guru, and drink in this water. Chanting and meditating forever on Guru Nanak, I live. || 4 || 43 || 56 ||

AUM

LAUGH!

Did you know, my Friend, that the Sage is generally laughing... According to the Enlightened, the best Laughter is at one's own self.

Blessed are they, who have learnt to laugh at themselves.

AUM

The Blank Page

Many, many, many Moons ago, narinder had posted on the Timeline the Story titled "The Blank Page"

narinder had said:

Each day you have been writing The Book of your Life; today is The Blank Page...

Write your story in such a way... give it a direction today... so that the Last Page of the Book has a joyous ending.

Early this Morning, Amritvela... The Guru opened in front of narinder Today's blank Page to write on...

At the end of the Day, narinder saw that the Page was still Blank... he was surprised... NO writing through-out the Day?

Then he turned to the previous Page... that too, was Blank... then a Page before... that too was Blank... and a Page before... Ah, it had contained the Ending... narinder had reached the Destination... the story had ended in Joy!!!

Each Day now comes to narinder, and will continue to come... till the ordained Day of Life in his Body... but there will be NO writing in each day... for his Page only reflects the Joy of Silence... NO Doing...

Much happens... but nothing is now narinder's Doing... all is done by God... narinder is only HIS instrument... the instrument of God's Law of Cause and Effect, which in fact IS God's Law of Love and Compassion.

AUM

THIS IS 'THE BLANK PAGE' for you to write your story on...

...as you wish to...

AUM

GOD it is, Who Plays the Other

... And then, makes the Other play

... Who sees in the Other... and makes the Other see.

HE it is, who speaks to the Other... and makes the Other speak;

He alone it is, who hears in the Other, and makes the Other hear...

HE is the Doer and Enjoyer in all...

Seated in the Heart/ Mind of the Other, exults and suffers...

Then one day, some day, decides that in that particular Other, HE has played enough;

And walks the Spiritual Path in the Other, makes the Other Meditate... and

Liberates the Self from the self... to abide in Bliss.

The Sage it is, who has realised the above... and is ever at Peace.

And in the Misery of suffering abide the Ignorant... NOT knowing who it is, Who is playing the Other.
AUM

Seven thousand Were the Tales narinder Read

Six Thousand knocked on his ears, to enthral

Five Thousand, he wrote, for the Joy of writing.

One fine morning, did the dawn dance its way to narinder's heart... to find...

The long Night's seven read, the six heard, the five sung...

Become, in an instant... just the Night's dream!

The Moon shyly hid her Face... the Sun smiled...

And narinder, the Lord's slave, laughed...

Oh, how the Beloved's eye gleamed...

... gleamed with Pride at HIS Creation!

AUM

Ah, Friend... In the Now... You were Born...

In the Now... you are Twenty and Two... (smile)

In the NOW, will the Eighty arise...

When every birth is the Birth in Now, and every death, a Death in Now...

How then, to pass any judgement on anything?

To Drop Concepts and Beliefs IS Enlightenment...

AND YET, narinder shall not disagree with blessed You, wise beyond your years, if you disagree with narinder.

You say, "You are as Young as You Think you are!"

Yes, Indeed!

amen, ameen

"What Fools these Mortals be!", laughs the Beloved, "But they are they, because I WILL them so to be! Oh, How I love them!"

AUM

Fear of Failure has Thee in Thrall...

Get over it... run not away from the challenges of Life...

Face them... and to help you face them, Pray to God and Meditate...

Be not daunted... succeed you will, whatever be the Odds...

There is NO such thing as Failure, narinder...

Failure is ONLY a step to success... shed your Fear... and take the step...

So what if you fail... so what! Heavens will Not Fall... NEVER!

Success is your Destiny! So said the Buddhas!

AUM

'Love gives... but Being Used Doesn't feel Sensational'

Many feel they are being, or have been, 'Used'.

The feeling of 'Being Used' is the Problem of 99.999%.

And the 0.0001%, (One in a Million), who gets enlightened NEVER feels any Problem whatsoever!

He does not say "being used doesn't feel sensational".

A very HIGH degree of Consciousness, many have achieved, dear Friends... through HIS Grace... now get ready to enter yet higher and higher levels of Consciousness...

For that the conditions are: You choosing so... Meditating more and more deeply... dissolving your 'i-ness' (ego) more and more...

Say Yes... right Now. The Lord awaits only your consent.

AUM, AMEN, AMEEN

Isn't Relationship a Two-Way Street?

narinder, one day asked Nari, Isn't Relationship a two-way street, Nari?

No, narinder, replied Nari, Not at all... Those who believe it so, only keep hurting themselves.

Only He/ She is Blissful, who decides to make it a One-way Street... and keeps serving others with love, without any expectation in Return.

Indeed, for the Realised One, when all is One and there is no Other, where is the question of a Two-Way street?

Once again 99.999% believe in the first Dictum... that Relationship is a Two-way street... and suffer much in their lives...

If you want to make the Right Understanding your way of life, narinder, if you want to flow with Unconditional Love, you will have to Meditate.

AUM

WHERE can You go Back,

Dear narinder... Where?

Neither Back... nor Forward can you go... O Immovable One...

The Self is everywhere and Nowhere... NOW HERE...

There is NO going back, or forward from Now and Here!

We co-exist... in this Now and Here... even though the sages realise that we exist not!

AUM

THE FINAL BEATITUDE

Na kuchh hoya, na kuchh hog [Nothing ever did happen, Nor shall it ever happen] ~ Nanak

This magnificence of your striving, this might of your endeavour - In Truth, nought was then happening... No Hope there be in Time for its flowering.

Nothingness it is that reigns in Time and Space
Nothingness that blows its Trumpet in the Void it rules.

It is to Nothingness that narinder bows, in Nothingness take refuge.

To Nothingness offer worship, Nothingness invoke; awaiting in anticipation
For Nothingness to reciprocate with forgiveness, mercy, and Love
To become, what it never was not... narinder's own self and being.

Aum.

How can pure Nothingness be spoken about or envisioned?
To lead some narinder into experience of Nothingness, some words/ boundaries are needed...
Nanak provides us the words... "Na kuchh hoya, na kuchh hog"...
But to experience this Truth, narinder needs to meditate... meditate... meditate...
AUM

The Beloved Bestowed...

The Beloved Bestowed on narinderness
... a Needle-point's Space in the Nothingness...
And, Nothingness did narinder become! Swiftly did he
become so... aye!

*Swift is this Mind... in a moment, it can travel the four corners
of the Universe. Faster than the Mind is THAT, the Self. ~~ ISA
Upanishad*

A Follow-Up on the Above:

Does it mean, narinder, that the Self is ever in a state of
Motion, like the Mind IS, ever beating the Mind in the Race?

Wow, Nari... truly, how swift the Mind must be!

YET, narinder... the Knowers have said 'the Self is Stillness
itself; It neither goes nor comes...'
Ah, Nari... you are Good at confusing everyone... very very
Good!!!

Nari only smiled... the Beloved laughed!

AUM

AH! SHAKESPEARE! And...
The Buddhas of Yore

To-morrow, and to-morrow, and to-morrow,
Creeps in this petty pace from day to day,
To the last syllable of recorded time;
And all our yesterdays have lighted fools
The way to dusty death. Out, out, brief candle!
Life's but a walking shadow, a poor player
That struts and frets his hour upon the stage
And then is heard no more. It is a tale
Told by an idiot, full of sound and fury
Signifying nothing.
~~Shakespeare's Macbeth (Act 5, Scene 5)

In Macbeth's final soliloquy, the audience sees Macbeth's final conclusion about life: that it is utterly devoid of any meaning, and that our days on this earth serve no purpose other than to lead us toward "dusty death".

Life is a seemingly endless and depressing succession of days creeping along at a bleak and "petty pace". Our time on this earth is so insubstantial that it can only be compared to a shadow or an illusion; so unreal that it can only be compared to a bad actor that worries and struts while onstage. When the play is over his character disappears into nothingness, and has left nothing significant behind.

Combine Shakespeare's wisdom with THAT of the Buddhas below... and you walk into Truth... the Bliss that Truth is.

The Alpha and the Omega...
The beginning and the end...
The Last word on Joy and Love
The ONLY worthwhile Understanding to imbibe
IS

The Path we walk IS of the self... by the self... for the self.

Once it takes hold of oneself, this Understanding...

Walking the Path in spite of it Being the Razor's Edge... becomes Easy.

"Becomes Easy" means that all the Buddhas, and the Masters, begin to send you their Blessings and an innate Strength...

Man, by himself, is always, too weak to walk this path of Discipline...

BUT, helped by God and the Masters, thousands have walked into the Liberation of non-duality... and have, in their turn, become Buddhas.

That you have begun to think so deeply on the subject, is itself a Proof of Grace... Blessed-ness!

Jai Jai Jai...

AND THUS IT IS... that the ONLY worthwhile Wisdom (in order to give meaning to Life) would be... to...

Meditate. Meditate. Meditate. ♥

Ah, My Beloved,
In Thee, I sought myself
Not then knowing that
It was in Me that
YOU were seeking Yourself!
~narinder

AUM

YOU don't Have to Worry, narinder

narinder wished the Ant a good Morning, and said "Take care, my friend, lest you get trodden under the big feet you are walking into."

And, he heard the Ant reply, "I don't have to worry, narinder. The Lord takes care of me, just as HE takes care of all creatures including you."

Then narinder saw the Ant return from under the feet of the elephant, bringing with it another Ant, who had lost its way.

Was narinder imagining it all... or was it the Truth?
He heard the Ant laugh. "No, narinder, you are not imagining it. What you just heard and saw IS indeed the Truth."

AUM

Humility in Others...

Everyone wants to humble Others... and to see Humility in Others...

narinder happened to meet the same Ant that he had met yesterday, and whose message, "I don't have to worry, narinder. The Lord takes care of me, just as HE takes care of all creatures including you" had humbled narinder; he wished the Ant Good Morning and said "O wise One, do you have a message for narinder today too?"

"Yes, if you please" said the Ant. "Everyone wants to humble Others... and to see humility in Others.

The Sage wants only to humble himself... and is watchful; he eradicates any traces of Arrogance, the Moment they raise their Head."

narinder bowed to the Wise Ant again.

AUM

Just Now,

O Vexed Spirit of the World...
Read the words of Ecclesiastes in the Holy Bible;
Read them WHENEVER your spirit is vexed . . . these words
of Ecclesiastes shall comfort you, like no other words...

Chapter 1
*Everything under the sun is vanity and vexation of spirit—He
who increases in knowledge increases in sorrow.*

1. *The words of the Preacher, the son of David, king in
    Jerusalem.*
2. *Vanity of vanities, saith the Preacher, vanity of vanities;
    all is vanity.*
3. *What profit hath a man of all his labour which he taketh
    under the sun?*
4. *One generation passeth away, and another generation
    cometh: but the earth abideth for ever.*
5. *The sun also ariseth, and the sun goeth down, and hasteth
    to his place where he arose.*
6. *The wind goeth toward the south, and turneth about unto
    the north; it whirleth about continually, and the wind
    returneth again according to his circuits.*
7. *All the rivers run into the sea; yet the sea is not full; unto
    the place from whence the rivers come, thither they
    return again.*
8. *All things are full of labour; man cannot utter it: the
    eye is not satisfied with seeing, nor the ear filled
    with hearing.*

9. *The thing that hath been, it is that which shall be; and that which is done is that which shall be done: and there is no new thing under the sun.*

10. *Is there any thing whereof it may be said, See, this is new? it hath been already of old time, which was before us.*

11. *There is no remembrance of former things; neither shall there be any remembrance of things that are to come with those that shall come after.*

12. *I the Preacher was king over Israel in Jerusalem.*

13. *And I gave my heart to seek and search out by wisdom concerning all things that are done under heaven: this sore travail hath God given to the sons of man to be exercised therewith.*

14. *I have seen all the works that are done under the sun; and, behold, all is vanity and vexation of spirit.*

15. *That which is crooked cannot be made straight: and that which is wanting cannot be numbered.*

16. *I communed with mine own heart, saying, Lo, I am come to great estate, and have gotten more wisdom than all they that have been before me in Jerusalem: yea, my heart had great experience of wisdom and knowledge.*

17. *And I gave my heart to know wisdom, and to know madness and folly: I perceived that this also is vexation of spirit.*

18. *For in much wisdom is much grief: and he that increaseth knowledge increaseth sorrow.*

AMEN

Ah, narinder,
The Simple Truth of Being...

The ocean, IF, you be...
The wave too you cannot NOT be...
Waves arise, waves subside,
Subside to arise again in the Ocean
Who is it who waves... or ocean be...
Is it the wave that 'ocean is'...
OR, is it the ocean, that 'waves'...

Ah, so simple is the understanding,
So effortless the 'knowing' -
You strive too much

That is your Bondage and Bane.
Drop all striving, allow Silence to arise...

BE....... Just Be .... and Smile

AUM

As One Grows in Stature...

As one grows in stature . . . one learns to de-centralise, to delegate things to be done to Others.

But some things cannot be delegated... like breathing, eating, taking medicine when sick, making love, and so on...

These acts are existential. Nature/ God requires them of the self.

narinder is reminded of a Joke he heard when a second-lieutenant in an Army Unit. The Commanding Officer asked his Adjutant, "Is sleeping with one's wife a Pleasure or a Duty?"
The Adjutant glibly replied, "It is a pleasure Sir. Otherwise you would have delegated it to me."

Meditation, too, cannot be delegated. It has to be done by the self. This Doing, this working on the self, invokes God/ Self to awaken you to the Fact that Meditation is your own Nature; your own Understanding and Bliss.

And, One more Thought. About Meditation.

Ah! 'I am' is only a Thought, and...
The THINKER, too
That, too, is a Thought!

MEDITATE... meditate... meditate...
And, Know... your own True state.

You, Sir, are neither the thinker, nor the thought
And, yet, you ARE...
You are the Thinker .... and, you are the Thought! (smile)

AUM

Here Now, For the Seekers of Truth:

Here now, for the Seekers of Truth, IS the complete information on Ego, and the Sun of Knowledge that eradicates Ego:

The ego... at least according to the teachings of Vedanta... isn't a bad thing to have.

The basic human ego condition in Vedanta is known as 'self-ignorance', or in Sanskrit 'ajnanam'.

It's important to note that self-ignorance is considered to be a condition of birth and not the fault of anyone who has it. Everyone, every single living being has self-ignorance, or that being wouldn't have been born in the first place. The only living beings that don't have self-ignorance are the ones who have self-knowledge. And these are considered to be quite, quite rare individuals.

What is the definition of the 'ego' in Vedanta. First of all it is known in Sanskrit as the 'ahankara', the aham 'I', kara 'maker'. The ego, or ahankara, is considered to be a type of thought, which is the hallmark of self-ignorance.

How does that 'thought' go? It goes, 'I am the doer, the thinker, the enjoyer'. In other words, 'I am the body/mind/sense organs individual, who does things, cognizes thoughts and objects, experiences pain and joy, and is subject to birth, death and change.'

Even for a person who has recognized the truth of existence there will still be an 'as though' ahankara. Otherwise that person couldn't get up, or eat, or walk, or talk, or do anything. There will still be an 'as though' identification with the body/mind for the purpose of functioning in duality, but this as though ahankara, or ego, is compared to a burnt rope.

If a rope lying on the ground is burnt, the shape will still be there, but that rope will no longer have the power to bind.

This is the same with the ego of a mature jnani —one who is firmly established in self-knowledge. He or she can still use the ahankara in order to function, but it no longer has the power to bind because that person has now recognized that the true identity of all things is the same.

That person knows, 'My existence is truly as the self – as the atma which is brahman unchanging, the ground of being. This is the truth of everything, and therefore my existence is not dependent upon a particular body/ mind/ sense organs individual in order to be.'

AUM

The Moment of Moments...

... For which long has been the wait...
The Wait now comes to an end... As the New Moment now
takes Birth.

A new day is dawning
With the subtle essence of the last twenty-four hours present
in it;
The New Moment is dawning
With the subtle essence of what the coming twenty-four hours
shall be.

The Yogi mounts astride the horse of the New Moment,
The Moment that the Lord has sent to him to ride.

The Moment of Moments, for which long has been the wait...
The Wait now comes to an end... As the New Moment now
takes Birth.

Smile, o narinder, for the past is dead... the future too...
Time is No More... even as a new Day begins to sing its Song.

AUM

I am Alone by Preference

The word 'Lonely' has an entirely different connotation.

Loneliness is the perpetual state of seeking that which one so craves, that which you so need.
Loneliness comes with settling for less than you deserve just as surely as it comes with reaching for that which you cannot attain. It's incurable by company, it swells in the presence of friends; it grips you unforgivingly, from within.

Whereas, Aloneness is strength. Aloneness is finding freedom in this very same isolation; it's the strange state of bliss that comes with being truly, honestly, unapologetically content in your own company.

[Photo pf the Alone Snow-wolf: Curtsy, Free Pixabay Photos]

AUM

This Brings You to the End of This Book.

Re –read this Book. Read it again and yet again...

Till the words you have read become your Silence, and the beginning of your reading of the Book of your own Life.

IF you have any doubts or questions on what you read, you may clarify the same from me, through my e-mail: narinder_bhandari@yahoo.co.in.

Aapo Deepo Bhava. Be your own Light.

Blessings of the Buddhas are with you.

AUM

PARTING ADVICE TO SEEKERS TRUE:

ONE:

Meditation, you will learn to DO, if possible directly from an Awakened Master.

The Two Books, you will EVER and EVER, keep reading, and reflecting on, will be

1. Bhagvad Geeta. The words 'Bhagvad Geeta' mean 'The Song sung to become ONE with the Lord'. You will read it always keeping that meaning in mind; not associating it with any Ism.
2. The Basic scripture of your own Religion.

These two books will be read again and again, till Awakening happens to you. Will be read even afterwards.

TWO:

Books to read in addition to the Basic Two above, as suggested by the Satguru (Only after your own Awakening):

1. 1.Ashtavakra Geeta.
2. Vivekachuramani by Shankra.
3. Patanjali's Yoga sutras.
4. Vedanta, including the various Upanishads.
5. Japji Sahib and Sukhmani Sahib... Nanak's Bani.
6. Nisargadatta Maharaj's Book "I am That"
7. Maharishi Ramanna's Book "Talks with Ramanna Maharishi"

8. "Siddhartha" by Herman Hess
9. "Jonathan Livingstone Seagull" by Richard Bach
10. Osho's Books on Zen

After your Awakening three Books will be your constant reading:

The two Basic Books suggested in ONE above.

Any ONE of the 10 Books given in TWO, serially one by one.

THREE:

After you have read and digested the Books in TWO above, more and more Books of Nisargadatta, Ramanna, Richard Bach, Upanishads and any spiritual Book, which God guides you to read... and, there will be many...

Links:

- To Japji Sahib, and Sukhmani Sahib:
  http://www.sikhs.org/english/eg1.htm
  http://www.sikhs.org/english/eg24.htm#p262
- Guru Granth Sahib: Gurmukhi script, and English.
  http://www.srigranth.org/servlet/gurbani.
  gurbani?Action=Page&Param=1
- OSHO'S Books, audios and videos:
  http://www.oshoworld.com/
  and
  http://www.oshoworld.com/discourses/audio_eng.
  asp?cat=D
- narinder's Writings in Facebook:
  https://www.facebook.com/narinder.bhandari

NOTE: There would be many commentaries available in the Market on each of the Books above. Nari (self) found the commentaries by Swami Chinmayananada and Osho Rajneesh to be the Best ..

Swami Chinmayananda's Triology, "Vedanta, the Science of Life" is excellent reading. Read each word of these three, with deep devotion.

Osho's Commentary on Japji Sahib, Bhagvad Geeta and Ashtavakra Geeta are superb. Audio Tapes are also available.

AUM _()_

Some Comments from readers:

To think BEYOND on GOD is certainly an art imbibed by a saint to know the SCIENCE BEYOND through one's sincere realization.

It is found well with our Blessed Realized person Narinder Bhandari. Not by name but by action he is a super-man, a treasure of Divine Realization, which being realized would be a service to the humanity at large.

I appreciate & congratulate the Yogi, to share his precious Divine experiences with the seekers."

~~ **Srividyaswami Mahamedhanandanath Saraswati: Bhubaneshwar-751030,(India)**

I highly recommend Narinder Bhandari's book. His teaching have opened my heart to a whole new Vista within, in deepening and touching Awareness within, these past several years.
Truly a transformational gift within this life.. Reading these words of wisdom and Insight, is opening me to a whole new level of understanding of what I Am..
A true blessing to have been drawn to such an inspirational, thoughtful guidance. Sheer grace!

Christine Ann Kauffman: Butte, Montana, USA.

The man, named ""Nari"" is a man, beyond life and death .....
he does not know how close 'HE' (God) is with him...

Nari can hear the voice of souls ... it does not mean that Nari
is a superman.... no no no!

... he, just is, a pure and holy human being.. He the Nari, is
like a innocent baby...and finally I would like say 'a child is
the very personification of God' so blessed....

With much Love Light & much blessings!!!

~~ **Dilip Kumar Vaidya (D K Vaidya Divyaguruji), Goa**

Bless you dearest friend Narinder.

What kind words which I am so happy and grateful to hear,
you're such an important person to whom I admire and
respect, please accept my apologies but know that you
have helped me so much to feel like my heavy burden has
lightened.

Thanks to you I do again feel able to pick myself up ready
for the new day and days ahead, you're indeed a great man
Narinder.

Please excuse my moment of weakness but know please how
humbly grateful I am to you.

Thanks so very much for everything, your reply, your words,
but most of all for being you, for you are aware and love flows
through your very veins.

~Your devoted friend always. Blessings I am so proud to know
you and to be able to call you my friend.

Nick Boswell.

London. U. K.

"Namaste beloved Narinder: My deepest love and respect to your blessed self. You are truly an enlightened Master. AUM AUM AUM.

OM SRI NARINDER BHANDARI NAMAH AUM. OM OM OM."

~ **Baba Nataraja (Swami Baba Nataraja Giri).**
Venice, California

Narinder Bhandari, 76, is a retired Army Officer, and lives in Chandigarh, INDIA with his wife Ravi, son Karan and family. The greatest 'happening' in his lifetime, says he, was "The Death of Time" for one single Moment in 1982; a gift of his Guru, God and Meditation. Past and Future ceased to exist. Life became a spontaneous living in the Light of awareness of the present Moment.

Printed in the United States
By Bookmasters